ROSWELL

ROSWELL

Uncovering the secrets of Area 51 and the fatal UFO crash

RUPERT MATTHEWS

CHARTWELL
BOOKS, INC.

Picture Credits

20ᵗʰ Century Fox Television/The Kobal Collection 188; AP/PA
Photos 176, 178; Bill Stoneham 16, 19, 38, 58, 69, 78, 94, 105,
125, 129, 130, 152, 165; Corbis 62, 103, 168, 175; Getty 84, 99;
Getty/AFP 180; JBColorado 187; Luke Jones 70; Mary Evans
Picture Library 29, 38, 41, 42, 43, 45, 47, 114, 142, 158; Matt
Beldyck 189; Photos.com 48; Qwerty Films/Warner Bros/The
Kobal Collection 155; Rebecca Glover 27 (2), 87, 89, 91, 92,
111, 121, 122, 123, 127, 148; Russell Smith 190; Shutterstock
30, 46, 74, 90, 93, 102, 119, 137, 151, 173; TopFoto 28;
TopFoto/Fortean 15, 20, 32, 34, 44, 50, 51, 52, 54, 67, 92, 112,
113, 115, 139, 143, 150, 162, 170.

This edition printed in 2009 by

CHARTWELL BOOKS, INC.
A Division of **BOOK SALES, INC.**
276 Fifth Avenue Suite 206
New York, New York 10001 USA

Copyright © 2009 Arcturus Publishing Limited
26/27 Bickels Yard, 151–153 Bermondsey Street,
London SE1 3HA

ISBN-13: 978-0-7858-2509-8
ISBN-10: 0-7858-2509-6
AD000392EN

Printed in China

Contents

Introduction

THE ROSWELL INCIDENT is, without doubt, the most famous UFO incident in the world. It is also the most controversial. Even among those who believe that alien spacecraft are visiting Earth, opinions are divided over what happened at Roswell.

Some hold firmly to the conclusion that an alien spaceship crashed near Roswell, New Mexico, in early July 1947. The wreckage and the remains of the dead crew were recovered under conditions of the tightest security by men of the United States Army Air Force (USAAF) and taken to the nearby Roswell Army Air Force base. From there they were transported to the top security research facility at Wright Air Field in Ohio for study. The experiments carried out at Wright Air Field have been responsible for producing all manner of modern high-tech products, including fibre-optics, the integrated circuit chip, lasers and a host of other objects.

Others believe that nothing very exciting happened at all. A weather balloon came down in the desert, got snagged on some scrub and was found by a ranch hand. An unfortunate series of misunderstandings then followed that created the illusion of a mystery where none existed. Thereafter, the event has been exploited by charlatans, fools and innocents to create an entirely false image of what was, in reality, an utterly dull event.

Within both camps there are divergent opinions and firmly held views. Indeed, one of the key distinguishing features of the Roswell Incident – unlike most other UFO-related events – is the sheer complexity of opinion and the dogmatic way in which those opinions are expressed. At times those studying the incident have been reduced to fairly unpleasant name calling when talking of each other. One researcher has accused another of lying, witnesses have been accused of being charlatans out to make a quick buck by inventing a far-fetched story, and even respected academics have been denounced as being either gullible or unwilling to accept evidence.

In large part all is a result of the nature of the evidence relating to the Roswell Incident. Unlike most UFO events that are discussed, there was no real research carried out at the time of the Roswell Incident by people interested in UFOs and keen to record as much detail as possible. Instead, evidence falls into four categories:

1) Contemporary written evidence that was published at the time. As we shall see this largely takes the form of newspaper articles, mostly in local or regional newspapers, though there were also a few references to events at Roswell in other publications at the time.

2) Contemporary written evidence that was not published at the time but which has been published since. This mostly takes the form of USAAF documentation relating to Roswell Army Air Force Base, the personnel stationed there and events that took place

there. A smaller quantity relates to FBI, police and other government agencies. At the time this mass of data was routinely kept secret, as most military documentation still is, but with the passing of time it has been declassified and made available to the public through the Freedom of Information legislation.

3) Contemporary written evidence that was not published at the time and which has still not been published. It is well known that much of the USAAF documentation relating to Roswell for the year 1947 has never seen the light of day. The reasons for this are varied. A large amount of it was destroyed at a time when it was thought to be no longer of any interest. Data pertaining to such mundane daily matters as the cookhouse food stores, for instance, are routinely incinerated by the military. Other documentation is known still to exist, but has not been released. Some of this is now available in second-hand and edited form as it features in official reports compiled by personnel who have had access to the original documents. Other documents remain completely secret. By their very nature, these documents represent a great unknown quantity. It is uncertain how many documents remain under wraps, still more vague is what they record.

4) The final and most prolific form of evidence is eyewitness testimony recorded some years after the Roswell Incident itself. Most of this testimony was recorded by UFO researchers during the 1980s and 1990s, though some evidence continues to turn up even today. Much of this evidence is first hand, but a fair amount of it is second hand. The quantity of this evidence is not in dispute, but the quality is. The human memory can play strange tricks as the years pass. Even a competent witness who is honestly doing his or her best to recall events accurately can make mistakes after an interval of 30 or 40 years – as most of those giving evidence about Roswell were doing. Of course, not all witnesses to events are as good as researchers would hope. Some may be tempted to exaggerate their claims to gain fame or to be able to charge a fee for giving interviews. It should come as no surprise that some witnesses to the events at Roswell contradict each other. This does not mean, however, that everything they say is misremembered or invented. Some of the statements may be false, some confused but some will be true and accurate.

This book sets out to find the truth behind the confusion that exists over the Roswell Incident. It does not take as its starting point any particular belief. There is no attempt to convince the reader that an alien spacecraft crashed at Roswell, nor that all the witness statements are untrustworthy. Instead it sets out to present the evidence for events in an impartial way and then allow the reader to draw his or her own conclusions.

Rupert Matthews, 2009

1
Frantic Days
in July

▶ A flight of piston-engined fighter aircraft of the 1940s. Although most aircraft in 1947 were powered by propellers, jet aircraft were entering service and there was much technological development going on.

WHATEVER IT WAS that happened at Roswell took place in the summer of 1947. The world was a very different place back then. The Second World War had ended only two years earlier, so people were still trying to adjust to peace and to the new shape of the world. People alive then knew things and took things for granted that today would seem odd or peculiar. Similarly there was a lot that we now accept as commonplace that would have seemed quite bizarre to a resident of a middle American town like Roswell in 1947.

Before embarking on a study of what did or did not happen at Roswell that summer, it is worth spending a bit of time reviewing the world as it appeared from Roswell at that time. The way in which the people of the town reacted to the events that unfolded that summer had much to do with how the world

seemed to them. Modern people would probably react quite differently, and the views and knowledge of the people of the time needs to be borne constantly in mind when reviewing the evidence. A person's behaviour that might strike us as odd or suspicious may have been perfectly natural in the 1940s.

The first thing to bear in mind is that Roswell was dominated by the nearby base of the United States Army Air Force (USAAF). The air force was, at the time, still officially part of the United States Army, as it had been for decades past. That would change before the end of 1947 when the United States Air Force (USAF) was born. Of course, the new organization was staffed by all the same men and women who had formed the USAAF. They were working on the same bases and doing the same jobs. However, there was a period of some months when administrative arrangements were changing over when some of the support staff and higher echelons of

▲ Although usually referred to as desert, the landscape around Roswell is more in the way of dry scrubland, which turns lush and green after the infrequent rains.

▶ An atomic bomb test in the late 1940s. It was thought by many at the time that UFOs were alien spacecraft attracted to Earth by the detonation of these bombs and the technological breakthrough by humans that they heralded.

command were in a state of flux. It was at this time, it is alleged, that some of the files relating to what had been the Roswell Army Air Force (RAAF) base but was now the Roswell Air Force (RAF) base got lost.

In itself, Roswell was a fairly typical small town of the date and place. Its location in south-eastern New Mexico put it in a somewhat remote area. The surrounding land was dominated by dry scrubland with intermittent pastures that made arable farming impossible, but made it good territory for livestock. Cattle roamed widely over the landscape, herded by a small number of ranchers and cowboys. The open country was very sparsely populated with the more arid areas barely being visited by humans at all.

Many of the jobs in Roswell depended on the presence of the military base. Anything likely to affect the base would affect the town, so the people may have been more interested in international or military events than the residents of other small towns. This is important as there were two events unfolding in the background that would have been known to all residents of Roswell and may well have affected their reactions to what happened.

INTERNATIONAL TENSION

The first of these was the international situation. The Second World War was over, but tensions with communist Russia were rising fast. Today we know that these tensions led to four decades of Cold War between the USA and Soviet Russia. We know that several small scale wars were fought in Korea, Vietnam and elsewhere that had as much to do with the superpower Cold War as with local antagonisms.

In 1947 nobody knew this. They did know that Soviet Russia was a hostile power of growing might and impressive military capability. It seemed likely then that the USA and Russia might face each other in open warfare

within a year or two. The most likely flashpoint would be in Europe, which was then recovering from having a savage war fought across it. Soviet tanks might roll into western Germany and France, with the USA and its allies responding in kind.

Soviet spies were known to be active in the USA. How many there were and how widespread their activities might have been was unclear. They may well have been active around any military base. But the USAAF base at Roswell was no ordinary base. It was a very special and secretive place indeed. It is not generally recognized today just how special the Roswell Army Air Force base was in the summer of 1947, but everyone living in Roswell would have known.

Stationed at RAAF was the 509th Bomber Group of the 8th USAAF. This was the only

It seemed likely then that the USA and Russia might face each other in open warfare within a year or two.

unit in the entire world that was trained, equipped and ready to deliver atomic bombs. This was only two years after the world's first atomic bombs had been dropped on Hiroshima and Nagasaki. The awesome power of the weapon was still new and deeply terrifying. And the bombs were almost unbelievably secret. Only the USA had atomic bombs, which gave them a huge military advantage over every other nation on Earth.

The citizens of Roswell were fully aware that they had the 509th based barely a ten-minute drive outside of their town. They knew that the 509th was the atomic bomb group. Even though they did not know the details of how many aircraft or atomic bombs were kept on site, the civilians of the area did know and understand the sensitive nature of the base. They knew also that it was their patriotic duty

▲ A view of the White Sands National Monument that gave its name to the nearby air base where a range of experimental weapons and aircraft were tested at the time of the Roswell Incident.

▲ Wernher von Braun (left) and Willy Ley prepare to watch the test firing of a US rocket. The testing of such top secret weapons and equipment was carried out at various bases in New Mexico.

to protect the air base and its many secrets.

Roswell was not the only top secret facility in the area. Several miles to the east was the White Sands base. Although named after the spectacular, pure white sand dunes that were something of a tourist attraction, the base covered a vast area of desert and arid scrubland that was of little use to the local ranchers. It was here that the USAAF was testing rockets.

Like the atomic bomb, the rocket was, in

1947, a new and terrifying weapon. It had first entered combat in the summer of 1944 when the Germans had launched hundreds of V2 rockets against London and adjacent areas of England. These rockets flew at supersonic speed, following a parabolic path high into the atmosphere. They could deliver a powerful charge of explosives on to their intended target. They could not be intercepted by fighters, nor could they be shot down by anti-aircraft guns. There was no defence against a rocket. Fortunately for the Londoners in 1944 the German rockets were unreliable, being prone to going off course in mid-flight or to blow themselves apart.

In 1945 the Americans had captured not only the German cache of unfired rockets but also their chief designer Wernher von Braun. Von Braun was now at work with a team of American engineers seeking ways to build bigger and better rockets that would be both more reliable and more accurate. These weapons were tested on the firing range of White Sands amid conditions of great secrecy.

But that was not all. Not far away was Los Alamos, the vast engineering facility that had been responsible for producing the first

◄ Colonel William Blanchard photographed at the time that he commanded Roswell air base in the late 1940s. It is alleged that he co-ordinated the cover-up of the UFO crash at Roswell.

atomic bombs. The test bomb had been detonated there early in 1945. In 1947 it was still operational as the scientists toiled to create better and more reliable atomic and hydrogen bombs.

All in all, this area of New Mexico was of enormous military significance. The civilians of the area may have had only the haziest idea of what was going on behind the locked

gates and guarded miles of fences, but they did know that it was of great importance to their nation.

Although the Roswell air base contained highly secret equipment, it was not entirely a closed base that had nothing to do with the town. The commander of the base, Colonel William Blanchard, was deeply concerned that the military should get on well with civil-

▲ An artist's impression of a typical alien encounter as reported by witnesses. The alleged spacecraft are often described as being smoothly rounded in shape and emitting light openings or portholes. The aliens that emerge are usually said to be between three and five feet (1–1.5 m) tall, with abnormally large heads and eyes.

ians. When he took up his post at Roswell he put his views into effect. His men were encouraged to go into town to socialize and mix freely with the local residents. Married personnel were encouraged to live off-base in rented houses in and around Roswell town. If the civilians ever wanted anything, Blanchard ordered that the military should help. Army trucks were loaned to ranchers; army jets performed fly-pasts for carnivals and fairs. Nothing was too much trouble.

Although civilians were not encouraged on to the Roswell air base, neither were they entirely banned. Several local businesses had contracts to supply services to it and their staff were regular visitors. Such staff had to undergo low-level security clearance and were issued with passes that allowed them on to the base.

Security was not compromised by the presence of civilians due to the fact that Roswell air base was divided internally into a series of compartments. The living quarters, cook-house, hospital and other facilities were located in a compound accessed directly from the main gate. It was to this compound that civilians had access. A secure fence separated this outer compound from the bulk of the base where the runway, aircraft and maintenance sheds were located. Only USAAF personnel had access to this area, the gates being guarded 24 hours a day by men who inspected the passes of anyone who wanted to enter.

Within this operational area there was a highly secure sector, which was patrolled by armed guards and surrounded by an impressive fence. Only a few personnel had security clearance to go in, and it contained the atomic bombs and other highly secret equipment that was stored on the base. If Blanchard was relaxed about access to the outer compound, his views on this inner section were very different. Security was paramount.

If the presence of the military in large numbers and highly secure guise was the first major background factor to the events of July

1947, the second was the growing awareness of an unease about flying saucers.

NEW TO UFOS

Today, the mention of 'UFOs' or 'flying saucers' brings with it a whole array of responses that would have been quite unheard of back in 1947. Most people today do not believe that UFOs are anything particularly exciting or interesting. Sightings do not make headline news on television or radio broadcasts and rarely even make it on to the inside pages of newspapers. So far as the media is concerned, the story is no longer of any real interest. If a person sees a strange object flying through the air that they cannot identify, it is no big deal. Hundreds of other people have seen similar things and nobody is any further forward in understanding what they are.

The general view among the media and the mass of the public is to accept that UFOs are seen from time to time. When the subject is given any thought at all, it is to suggest that most UFOs are perfectly mundane and normal objects seen under unusual circumstances that make them appear to be something bizarre. Any witnesses that talk about seeing diminutive humanoids emerging from a landed UFO are generally considered to have been hallucinating. There

Today, the mention of 'UFOs' or 'flying saucers' brings with it a whole array of responses that would have been quite unheard of back in 1947.

is no obvious answer to the question of what UFOs might be or what their occupants (if they exist) are after. Most people have enough problems in their lives without bothering about unproven claims of little green men running about the world. On the whole, the subject is consigned to science fiction novels and Hollywood blockbuster films awash with special effects.

Among those who have an interest in UFOs, on the other hand, views are very different. It is generally accepted that those UFOs that cannot be easily ascribed to natural phenomena are very real and solid objects. The most popular theory – although not the only one – is that they are mechanical flying devices, most likely being spaceships bringing aliens to Earth. There is no firmly held view as to where the aliens come from (though they are quite clearly not from this solar system) nor what they are coming to Earth for. The evidence is not clear-cut.

There have been a large number of sightings of what seem to be aliens that fit into what can be termed the 'scientist-explorer' category. These aliens land their UFOs in remote, usually rural areas, far from human habitation. They emerge from their craft to study wildlife and flora, often collecting samples of local wildlife, soil and rocks. When these beings become aware that a human has stumbled on to the scene they usually flee, scrambling into their vehicle and flying off at speed. Occasionally they react more aggressively. Some humans have found themselves attacked by beams of light that paralyze them or knock them unconscious. Such attacks are never followed up, and serve only to render the human immobile while the aliens get away.

According to witnesses, these aliens come in a variety of shapes and sizes, but the vast majority conform to a fairly standard description. They are said to be something less than 5 ft (1.5 m) in height and roughly of human appearance, though the heads are somewhat larger than might be expected of a human of the same height. The faces are sometimes described as being of a pinched appearance, with all the features squeezed into the lower half of the front of the head. The eyes are often said to be larger and more slanted than those of a human.

An altogether different type of alien encounter has been the alien abduction. These events have tended to dominate UFO research in recent years, so much so that some UFO researchers no longer bother with actual Unidentified Flying Objects. Unlike the 'scientist-explorer' aliens, the 'abductors' are not always seen with a UFO. Abductors may kidnap their victims from bedrooms as often as from roadsides. Once they have their human victim ensnared, the abductors take them to a chamber filled with medical instruments. This chamber is usually assumed to be on board a UFO, but this is not always clear. The unfortunate human is then subjected to a series of medical examinations, some of them excruciatingly painful, before being dumped back at the spot from which they were taken.

The aliens said to be responsible for these abductions are usually referred to by researchers as 'Greys'. They have skin of a pale grey or off-white colour; they have spindly limbs and short, thin bodies. Their heads, by contrast, are large and bulbous with tiny ears, noses and mouths. The most noticeable feature of the Greys is their eyes. These are said to be massive and totally black. Some witnesses say that the aliens communicate with them by what seems to be telepathic messages beamed through the eyes.

Such is the common view held of UFOs and aliens by the general public and dedicated researchers today. Back in 1947 things were very different indeed. The term 'Unidentified Flying Object' had not yet been coined. The strange objects seen flying through the skies were usually termed 'flying saucers' or 'flying disks'. And they were very newsworthy. Each new sighting was likely to be splashed over the headlines of the local media, with noteworthy examples dominating the national newspapers and radio broadcasts – television was then in its infancy.

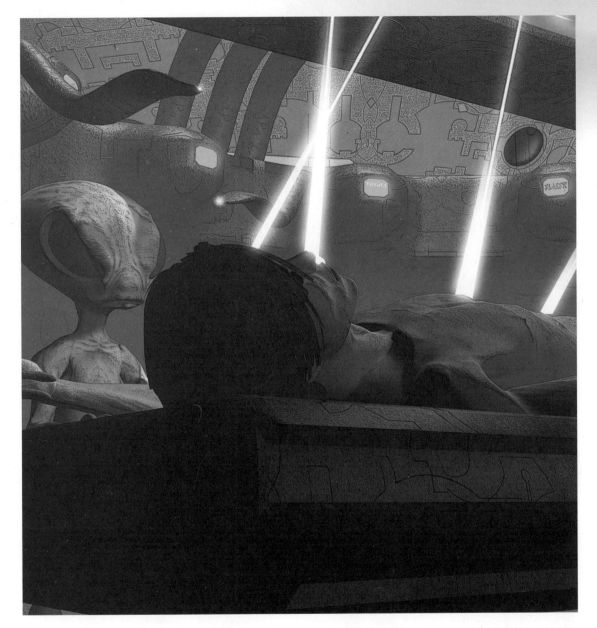

◄ Some people
who claim
to have
encountered
aliens say that
they were
abducted and
subjected to
unusual
procedures of
an apparently
medical nature.

THE FIRST ENCOUNTER

The first sighting to hit the headlines had taken place as recently as 24 June 1947, only a couple of weeks before the events unfolded at Roswell. Businessman Kenneth Arnold took a few hours off from a sales trip to Washington State to fly his private aircraft up over the Cascade Mountains to search for a US Marines transport aircraft that had gone missing and was presumed to have crashed in the area.

While searching around Mount Rainier, Arnold spotted a formation of nine strange aircraft. That the aircraft flew in an unusual formation was the first thing Arnold noticed. Military jets usually flew in echelon; the leading aircraft would be in front and low down with the following planes stacked up and to the side behind it. These flew in precisely the opposite formation, with the lead aircraft above those behind. As the aircraft came close, Arnold noticed that they lacked the tails that gave every normal type of air-

► Kenneth Arnold and his wife. It was Kenneth Arnold's sighting of unusually shaped, high speed 'flying saucers' that sparked interest in unexplained flying objects in 1947.

craft its stability in flight. Indeed, these machines seemed to relish a lack of stability because they skipped, weaved and bobbed along as they flew. Arnold later likened the motion to 'like a saucer would if you skipped it across water' – which gave rise to the term 'flying saucer'.

Arnold also noticed the excessive speed of the objects – he estimated it to be around 1,200 mph (1,900 kph), far faster than any aircraft Arnold knew of. Not only that, but they had a very unusual shape. As well as not having a tail, the aircraft lacked any clear definition between fuselage and wing. They were shaped rather like truncated crescents with the tips of the crescents being the wings and the centre being the fuselage.

Deeply puzzled, Arnold flew on to land back home at Pendleton, Oregon. By the time he got there he had reached a number of conclusions regarding the odd flying machines that he had seen. Firstly they were utterly unlike any aircraft or missile that he had seen or even heard of. Secondly, any country that had such aircraft

would possess a great advantage in either commerce or warfare over its rivals. Arnold went to see the FBI because, as he said later: 'I kind of felt I ought to tell the FBI because I knew that during the war we were flying aircraft over the pole to Russia and I thought these things could possibly be from Russia.'

When he arrived the FBI office was shut as all the local agents were out on investigations. In the time he spent waiting for them to come back, Arnold spoke to some journalists and told them what he had seen. One of them latched on to Arnold's saucer analogy and dubbed the objects 'flying saucers'. Although the term actually referred to the motion of the objects in flight, most newspaper readers assumed it referred to their shape and imagined the objects to be circular even though Arnold was clear that they had been crescent-shaped. The misunderstanding would later prove to be crucial at Roswell.

Arnold's story flashed across America and hit the national headlines. Most reporters followed Arnold's idea that these mysterious objects were mechanical aircraft from a foreign country, most likely from Russia – though a few noted the site's proximity to Canada and wondered if the British were up to something.

A RASH OF SIGHTINGS

In the days that followed a number of other people reported seeing the flying saucers. The best-known of these was by United Airlines pilot E.J. Smith and co-pilot Ralph Stevens, who, on 4 July 1947, sighted craft very similar to those seen by Kenneth Arnold. Smith was a well-known pilot of proven steady nerves and good eyesight, so his report was treated very seriously. By the end of July around 850 sightings of flying saucers had been made in the USA. A good many of these could, with hindsight, be written off as sightings of conventional aircraft seen by untrained observers or of natural phenomena such as meteors, but many could not. In any case, they were taken seriously at the time.

So far as the residents of Roswell (both civilian and military) were concerned, the flying saucers were very real indeed. They had started to be seen only a few weeks earlier, but now were appearing in ever larger numbers. They were not American, yet they were apparently invading American air space with impunity. Most people thought that they were aircraft of some revolutionary new design. It was only two years since rockets and jets had become known in public, both inventions that easily outstripped the conventional propeller-driven aircraft of the time. Now it seemed that somebody had come up with something that outperformed jets and rockets with equal ease.

Some thought the unknown inventor might be a super-rich and secretive American corporation or individual. Others suggested that the USAAF itself had developed the astonishing new machines. Most worried it was the Russians who were responsible.

Then a pattern began to emerge in the sightings. By 1 July it was noticed that more sightings were taking place over the arid states of the south-western USA than elsewhere. Those looking for a reason why the saucer pilots might be so interested in Arizona, New Mexico and adjacent areas did not have far to look. It was here that the atomic bomb had been developed, here that missiles were being tested and here that the 509th Bomber Group was based at Roswell. Speculation in local bars, shops and newspapers had it that the saucer pilots were spying out America's atomic secrets.

This was the background against which the events of July 1947 were played out. Of course, the vast majority of people were busy with their own daily lives. Cattle and sheep needed caring for, children had to go to school, paperwork had to be completed and

so forth. Thoughts of Russian spies, flying saucers and military secrets were rarely in the forefront of anybody's mind that hot summer, but everyone knew about them and would react accordingly.

The first indication to the outside world that anything odd had happened at Roswell came on Tuesday 8 July 1947 when the *Roswell Daily Record* and several other New Mexico evening newspapers carried a story based on a press release issued by Lieutenant Walter Haut, the public information officer at Roswell air base. No copy of the original press release issued by Haut has survived, but the Association Press (AP) bulletin based on it that was sent out over the wire service to all

> **Speculation in local bars, shops and newspapers had it that the saucer pilots were spying out America's atomic secrets.**

subscribing newspapers and radio stations has survived. In journalistic jargon of the time a 'bulletin' was a message of the highest importance. Ranked slightly below a bulletin was a 'code 95' message. Beneath that came an 'update'.

The bulletin was sent out at 2.26 pm Roswell time and read as follows:

Roswell, N.M. – The army air forces here today announced a flying disc had been found on a ranch near Roswell and is in army possession.

The Intelligence office reports that it gained possession of the 'Dis' through the cooperation of a Roswell rancher and Sheriff George Wilson of Roswell.

The disc landed on a ranch near Roswell sometime last week. Not having phone facilities, the rancher, whose name has not yet been obtained, stored the disc until such time as he was able to contact the Roswell sheriff's office.

The sheriff's office in turn notified a major of the 509th Intelligence Office.

Action was taken immediately and the disc was picked up at the rancher's home and taken to Roswell Air Base. Following examination, the disc was flown by intelligence officers in a Superfortress (B-29) to an undisclosed "Higher Headquarters".

The air base has refused to give details of construction of the disc or its appearance.

Residents near the ranch on which the disc was found reported seeing a strange blue light several days ago about three o'clock into the morning.

Ends.

AN AMBIGUOUS REPORT

Several things about this initial news alert should be noted. Firstly there are some elementary mistakes that would be corrected in later updates. The object is referred to as a 'Dis', not a 'Disk'. Also, the name of the Roswell sheriff was George Wilcox, not George Wilson. Such errors were not particularly unusual in a first bulletin of a breaking story and it was normal for them to be corrected quickly.

Secondly there are some ambiguities. The date on which the flying disk was said to have crashed was given as 'sometime last week', which might mean any date from Monday 30 June to Sunday 6 July. The site of the crash was given as only 'a ranch near Roswell', though the remoteness of the ranch was emphasized so presumably it was not too near.

Finally, some confusion has been caused by the fact that the remains of the crashed disk were said to be on board a 'Superfortress (B-29)'. This referred to the heavy bomber aircraft with which the 509th was equipped, and several of which had been specially adapted to carry atomic bombs. For the time it was a huge craft with a wing span of 141 ft (43 m), a length of 99 ft (30 m) and a weight in excess of 40 tons (36 tonnes). It was powered by four mighty Wright R-3350-23 engines, each capable of delivering 2,200 horsepower to the propellers they powered. Its defensive armament was impressive, consisting of 12 0.5 inch (13 mm) machine guns and a 20 mm cannon, but its main purpose was to carry a bomb load of 20,000lb (9,000 kg) over a range of 2,000 miles (3,200 km) at speeds of up to 320 mph (515 kph). It was an awesome weapon of war.

The confusion has arisen over why wreckage of anything, still less of a flying saucer, should be loaded on to a bomber. It has generally been assumed that this was done because the 509th had dozens of these mammoth aircraft and that no smaller plane was available. Others have suggested that the use of a heavily armed bomber indicated that the wreckage was considered to be very important, and even that the aircraft carrying it might come under attack.

In fact the 509th also had a number of B-29 aircraft that had been adapted for use as transports. These aircraft had their guns and bomb bays removed to be replaced by a flat-floored cabin that ran along much of the fuselage. They could carry large, heavy loads over considerable distances. For the 509th they were invaluable. If a war were to start, the 509th was under orders to move immediately to one of a number of prearranged air bases from where their bombers would be in range of the enemy country. The huge transports were designed to shift the vast array of maintenance and other equipment needed to keep the bombers in the air and their crews in top condition. It is likely that a B-29 transport was chosen simply because it was available and ready to fly.

Four minutes later an update went out. This named the public information officer at Roswell air base as 'Lt Warren Haught',

▲ The crew of a
B-29 bomber
test equipment
before closing the
hatch that will
keep their
compartment
pressurized at
high altitude,
a highly advanced
feature of aircraft
design at the
time.

◀ A B-29 bomber
of the type that
was based at
Roswell in
1947. At the
time, these
were the
mainstay of
the strategic
bomber force
of the USAAF.

▲ The Pentagon, central headquarters of the American military, in Washington DC. The initial official reaction to the breaking Roswell story was handled here.

another mistake that was soon to be corrected. It repeated that the object had been found 'sometime last week' and some other information. It also named (correctly) the Roswell intelligence officer handling the case as 'Major Jesse A. Marcel' and went on to say: 'The disc was picked up at the rancher's home. It was inspected and subsequently loaned by Major Marcel to higher headquarters.' The bulletin was then repeated on the AP international wire service, alerting reporters around the world to the news that a flying disk had been captured at Roswell.

A few minutes later there came another update that contained the sort of operational information that all reporters need. The contact at the Pentagon in Washington DC for reporters was to be Lieutenant General Hoyt S. Vandenberg, deputy chief of the army air forces.

If the earlier bulletin about the capture of a flying saucer was not enough to get reporters around the country interested, then the operational note was guaranteed to do so. A lieutenant general was a very high ranking officer indeed in anyone's language. If a man of such exalted rank as Hoyt Vandenberg was taking personal charge of the press for the

USAAF units in the Mediterranean theatre, again being decorated, this time with the Silver Star and the Distinguished Flying Cross.

His career thus far had been spectacularly successful, but conventional. Then, in 1946, he was appointed to be Director of Intelligence at the War Department. The role not only gave him contacts in government as well as the military – it also gave him unlimited access to the secret intelligence files maintained by the entire military. On 15 June 1947, a date that would later acquire some significance in the Roswell Incident, Vandenberg became the Deputy Commander of the USAAF.

PRESS EXCITEMENT

Any newshound hearing that Vandenberg was taking personal charge of the press on a story would immediately conclude that the story was of the utmost importance. That, indeed, seems to be what happened. At 3.10 pm a new bulletin went out on the AP wire service to all reporters – presumably in response to an avalanche of phone calls. This stated that AP reporters were 'going after the story' and that more details would be released as soon as possible.

Two minutes later another update was put out on the AP wire to say that General Vandenberg had issued a statement from the Pentagon. It proved to be a bit of a disappointment to the reporters who snatched it from the wire service:

'The War Department has nothing to say immediately about the reported find.'

If the earlier bulletin about the capture of a flying saucer was not enough to get reporters around the country interested, then the operational note was guaranteed to do so.

story, then it must be considered by the USAAF to be of the highest priority.

Vandenberg was, in fact, no ordinary lieutenant general – if there is such a thing. Born in 1899, Vandenberg joined the USAAF in 1923 and was commissioned as an officer to fly with attack squadrons, known in Britain as fighter squadrons. He then began a meteoric rise up the chain of command so that by the time the USA entered the Second World War he was operations and training officer of the Air Staff – performing the task so well that he was awarded the Distinguished Service Medal. In 1943 he took over as Chief of Staff for all

replied that he could give out no further information until he had been authorized to do so.

Those unable to get through to Haut began calling the sheriff's office. Soon the phone lines there were jammed as well, which did not please Sheriff Wilcox, as he had a job to do. The quantity of calls pouring in was soon so great that no calls could be placed out of Roswell. There were, after all, only a few wires strung out across the miles of grazing scrub and desert linking Roswell with the outside world. In the days before fibre optics and mobile phones there was a limit to what a phone network could do. That limit was reached at Roswell that afternoon.

Meanwhile, the local newspapers and radio stations – whose reporters had the enormous benefit of being on the spot and so were not reliant on phone lines – had gone to work. They had quickly established that the unnamed rancher on whose land the flying saucer had crashed was William Brazel, who worked the Foster Ranch. This ranch was not actually at Roswell at all, but some 80 miles (130 km) to the north-west near the township of Corona.

It was not the most prosperous of ranches, but Brazel earned a reasonable living from the cattle and sheep that he ran. The ranch house – long since demolished – was a simple wood and adobe building with assorted outbuildings, but no electricity and no running water. Brazel's wife and two younger children lived in Tularosa where the kids went to school. His eldest son, William Junior, lived and worked in Albuquerque, about 120 miles (190 km) away. He was only recently married and had moved out of the family home barely a year earlier. Although they were scattered across the state, the family remained fairly close and got together whenever possible.

The older Brazel was almost universally referred to as 'Mac', so much so that many people thought that was his name. In fact it was a nickname that originated when he was a

Presumably Vandenberg was waiting until he had more definite information before going public.

Not content with the assurances from the AP, and frustrated by Vandenberg's terse statement, reporters from across the USA, and soon after from around the world, began trying to 'go after the story' themselves. The first target for their calls was Lt Walter Haut, but his phone was soon jammed. To all calls, Haut

William 'Mac' Brazel as he appeared in 1947 when working on the ranch.

toddler when he was thought to resemble in comical fashion the then president, William McKinley, who was also known as Mac.

Those who knew him would often term Mac Brazel 'an old-time cowboy'. He was widely regarded as being honest and dependable, highly skilled at his work and unassuming. The general opinion was that if he said something, then it could be relied upon to be true – at least to the limit of Brazel's knowledge. He was not given to making things up or exaggerating.

None of the local newspapers carried an interview with Brazel about his find, nor even a direct quote. The reason for this was that they could not find him. Brazel was with the military, helping them with their inquiries. The *Roswell Daily Record* did, however, have a photo of him on file and this was quickly sent

The ranch worked by Brazel was little more than a wooden shack with associated buildings. There was no running water, no telephone and no power.

over the wire to appear in newspapers across the state. The photo showed Brazel in his high-crowned cowboy hat with curled brim. His shirt was open at the neck as he smiled rather uncertainly at the camera.

The *Roswell Daily Record* also uncovered some other details. The flying saucer had, apparently, already left Roswell and was on its way to 'higher headquarters'. The newspaper also covered a related story. Mark Sloan, who ran the private Carrizozo flying field, reported that his airfield had been buzzed by a flying saucer the day before. The saucer had been seen by himself, flying instructor Grady Warren and two pilots, Nolan Lovelace and Ray Shafer. The object had been travelling at about 200 mph (320 kph) and was heading north-west – towards the Foster Ranch.

The New Mexico radio stations were agog with the story. Normal programmes were interrupted with frequent updates on the breaking story. Reports of UFO activity across the state came in by telephone from farmers, housewives and others. It began to seem as if something hugely important and not a little sinister was going on. With one saucer down, apparently crashed and captured by the USAAF, and other saucers hurtling around in some numbers, the situation did not look good. Were the saucers searching for their downed comrade? Were they massing for an attack on the USAAF that had captured their colleague? Would civilians get caught up in a battle between the USAAF and the mysterious saucers? And were they from Russia, Britain or elsewhere? Nobody knew, but everyone was glued to their radios.

One man who was listening eagerly was a Canadian RAF officer named Hughie Green, who was later to become a well-known television entertainer in Britain. He was driving across New Mexico at the time on private business and had his car radio tuned in to the local stations to help pass the time during the long, lonely drive. During the recently ended war, Green had flown several combat missions over Germany and had experienced his own UFO sighting in the course of one such flight.

▶ British TV personality Hughie Green was hugely popular in the 1950s and 1960s. His testimony would prove to be crucial in uncovering the Roswell story.

Foo Fighters

Of course, in 1944, the objects Hughie Green had seen had not been called either UFOs or flying saucers. They had been known as 'foo fighters'. These objects took the form of glowing balls of light during the hours of darkness that were about 8 to 10 ft (2.5 to 3 m) across. During the day they appeared to have a dull, metallic sheen. Both by day and by night the foo fighters behaved in a similar way. They would come seemingly from nowhere to fly alongside an aircraft, often as close as 20 ft (6 m) or so away. After escorting the aircraft for a while, the foo fighters would abruptly change course and fly off out of sight at high speed.

When they first started appearing in the war-torn skies over Europe, the aircrew who saw them thought that they were some kind of new German secret weapon. It was expected that the foo fighters might suddenly ram Allied aircraft, or manoeuvre in close before exploding and bringing the Allied aircraft down. But this did not happen, so a new theory arose that the foo fighters were some

sort of automatic flying device that homed in on aircraft, sending out a transmission that allowed the German fighter pilots to close in for an easy kill. When German fighters failed to arrive in the wake of the foo fighters, this idea was also discarded. Some air gunners took to taking potshots at any foo fighters that came too close, but so far as is known none were ever shot down.

After the war ended, technical experts from both the RAF and the USAAF hurried to seize the technical research papers and scientists that had been producing the German aircraft and air weapons. They were amazed to find that the foo fighters had not been a German device at all. Indeed, German aircrew had also

▲ Foo fighters fly alongside a military aircraft in World War II. The identity of these odd, miniature flying disks has never been discovered.

It was expected that the foo fighters might suddenly ram Allied aircraft, or manoeuvre in close before exploding and bringing the Allied aircraft down.

been bothered by the objects and had come to the conclusion that they were some fiendish Allied device. The mystery of the foo fighters was never solved, so Hughie Green listened eagerly to the radio broadcasts about the captured saucer at Roswell in the hope that it would finally answer his questions about what he had encountered three years earlier over Germany.

Meanwhile, the mysterious 'higher headquarters' to which the flying saucer had been transferred was revealed to be Fort Worth Army Air Field, just outside Fort Worth, Texas. As yet only the local media in Fort Worth was aware of this as the announcement came in the form of telephone calls to them from the office of Brigadier General Roger Ramey, com-

> **The precise timing of the events that followed at Fort Worth Air Field has been analyzed in great detail.**

mander of the 8th USAAF, which included the 509th at Roswell. The news was not put out on the AP wire nor was it announced officially from Washington at this point.

The phone calls were made at about 3.10 pm Roswell time, which was 4.10 pm in Fort Worth. Reporters were summoned to a press conference about the captured flying saucer to be held at Fort Worth Air Field at 4.45 pm (3.45 pm in Roswell). That did not leave much time for the reporters to get out of town and in the rush only one, Bond Johnson of the *Fort Worth Star*, managed to grab a camera with film and flash light.

The precise timing of the events that followed at Fort Worth Air Field has been analyzed in great detail and there are some discrepancies between the different versions, but the outline is clear. Some of this confusion has no doubt been caused by the fact that local time in Fort Worth is one hour ahead of local time in Roswell. For ease of reference,

this book uses Roswell time throughout. It was also the case that the reporters were in a state of high excitement, each eager to get the scoop of the year ahead of his rivals. It is unlikely that any of them made a careful note of the precise time at any stage in the events. This has proved to be most frustrating for later UFO researchers, but was understandable at the time.

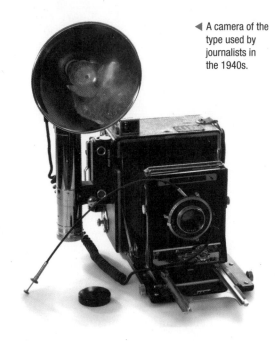

◀ A camera of the type used by journalists in the 1940s.

RUSH OF REPORTERS

The first reporters began arriving at about 3.30 pm. They were met at the gate by orderlies who escorted them to the building where General Ramey had his office. This caused some surprise as there was a dedicated and purpose-built press room in which press conferences were usually held. At around 3.45 pm, most of the reporters summoned had arrived and were ushered towards Ramey's office. They were told that the wreckage of the saucer was in the room.

General Ramey told the assembled reporters that the 'saucer wreckage' had now been firmly identified as being the remnants of a weather balloon. Ramey then introduced his adjutant, Colonel Thomas DuBose, who gave further details of the type of balloon that had allegedly been recovered. Another officer was then introduced as Major Marcel (who had flown in with the wreckage from Roswell), while a warrant officer was introduced as Irving Newton, the meteorological officer at Fort Worth.

The four USAAF personnel then led the reporters into Ramey's office. Johnson was allowed to shoot several photos of the material and the servicemen. The reporters fired off questions, which Ramey answered, or passed on to DuBose and Newton. Marcel was not called upon to answer any questions by Ramey and remained silent throughout. DuBose answered general questions about events to date, while Newton was called upon to identify the debris as that of a Rawin target balloon, a type of high altitude balloon that carried meteorological instruments high into the sky to collect data. He pointed out various features of the wreckage that confirmed this identification. At about 4 pm the reporters left the room and hurried off to return to their offices.

While all this had been going on, the AP wire service had carried a news update at 3.53 pm. This came from the Pentagon but was issued in the name of the same General Ramey who was at that very moment busy talking to reporters in Fort Worth. The usual explanation for this is that Ramey had sent the message to Vandenberg before the reporters arrived, but that Vandenberg had waited some twenty minutes or so before issuing it to the press.

The update stated that the wreckage of the saucer that had crashed at Roswell had arrived in Fort Worth and been inspected by Ramey. It had then been flown on immediately to Wright Air Field in Ohio.

By itself the statement made perfect sense, as it did to all those reporters outside Fort Worth who were unaware of what was taking place in Ramey's office. Ramey and the headquarters staff of the 8th USAAF in Fort Worth were an operational unit. They had all the skills needed to bomb enemy bases and protect their own, but they were not equipped to deal with a mysterious and unidentified crashed flying saucer. The Foreign Technology Division based at Wright Air Field, however, was. It was a top secret research group dedicated to studying any aircraft or air weaponry from other countries that fell into the hands of the USAAF. It was clearly imperative in a war situation that pilots should know how fast enemy aircraft could fly and the capabilities of their weapons. The team there must have been itching to get their hands on a flying saucer

Newton was called upon to identify the debris as that of a Rawin target balloon, a type of high altitude balloon that carried meteorological instruments

ever since Kenneth Arnold had reported his first sighting. It was the natural place to send a flying saucer should one be captured.

When Johnson got back to his office, he hurried to get his photos processed. The AP staff in Fort Worth had heard that he had gone to Fort Worth Air Field with a camera and was even then arriving with a portable photo transmitter that was able to reduce a photo to coded information that could then be transmitted over the wire and reassembled at any receiving station.

At 4.30 pm Major Edwin Kirton, the intelligence officer of the 8th Air Force at Fort Worth, issued a statement that declared the supposed saucer to be 'a Rawin high-altitude sonding device'. The statement got no further than the local media. It was overtaken by the exciting news that General Ramey would make

a live announcement on radio about the captured saucer. The broadcast would be made over the National Broadcasting Company (NBC) network, courtesy of the Fort Worth-based WBAP radio station and its studios.

VANDENBERG STATEMENT

At 4.59 pm the AP wire service carried an alert from Washington telling reporters that a major new development in the story was expected. This was, presumably, following an announcement from Vandenberg's office that an important official statement was about to be made. The statement did not come out over the AP wire until 5.29 pm. It began:

Roswell's celebrated 'flying disk' was rudely stripped of its glamor by a Fort Worth army airfield weather officer, who late today identified the object as a weather balloon.

A Dead Story?

Across the nation interest in the story died rapidly. On 9 July Hughie Green reached his destination and dashed out to buy the morning papers. There was nothing in them about the captured flying saucer. This puzzled him as the radio stations in New Mexico the previous day had talked about nothing else. A few newspapers elsewhere carried the USAAF explanation that the crashed saucer had, in fact, been a weather balloon, but only as a small story on inside pages.

Back in Roswell, the media was not as willing to forget the story as were the newspapers elsewhere. On 9 July the *Roswell Daily Record* carried the official story prominently on the front page, complete with coverage of Ramey's radio broadcast and a brief résumé of the original story in case any reader had missed it. There was an accompanying interview with Mac Brazel. In the course of the short interview, Brazel told how he had found the debris on his ranch a few days earlier and that he now accepted the official version of the story. But he concluded with the following:

> *I've seen weather balloons before and I am sure what I found was not any weather observation balloon. But if I find anything else besides a bomb, they are going to have a hard time getting me to say anything about it.*

The story went on to review events to date, then repeated Newton's firm identification of the debris that he saw in Ramey's office as coming from a weather balloon. Not noticed at the time was the fact that Newton said the debris was the remains of a 'Rawin target balloon', not a 'Rawin sounding device' as claimed by Kirton. Again the discrepancy would, years later, acquire a significance that it did not have at the time.

They had all the skills needed to bomb enemy bases and protect their own, but they were not equipped to deal with a mysterious and unidentified crashed flying saucer.

Leased Wire

Associated Press

Roswell Daily

VOL. 47. NUMBER 100 ESTABLISHED 1888   ROSWELL, NEW MEXICO, WEDNESDAY, JULY 9, 1947

Gen. Ramey Empties Ro

Lewis Pushes Advantage in New Contract

Southern Mines Only Hold-outs In New Contract

Washington, July 9, (AP) — The odds lengthened today that John L. Lewis would play his new, ace-studded contract into a grand slam.

With 75 per cent of the soft coal industry signed up for work and shooting at full production by tomorrow, Southern operators still held out against the unprecedented wage pact signed yesterday by most Northern and Western producers.

The Southern Coal Producers association prepared to make its "final decision" at a noon meeting today. Its 100,000 workers are idle.

But one association member acknowledged privately that it looked as though, sooner or later all would be "forced" to accede. Lewis, it was learned, rejected their request to alter some of the terms in a 90-minute session yesterday.

Federal labor officials conceded it would be difficult for the South to hold out alone, with the rest of the country producing and selling coal—at a price perhaps 70 cents to $1 a ton higher than before.

Lewis proclaimed his own certainty of the outcome.

It is "reasonable to assume," he said, after telling reporters of the United Mine Workers' fat contract gains, that the rest of the industry will sign up in a few days.

He indicated a resolve to smash the Southern association, his bitterest industry antagonist in recent years. Terming it purely a "propaganda agency" with which the UMW need not deal, Lewis said any of its 13 member associations may sign up independently.

Besides the unprecedented concessions—a 44 1/2 cent basic hourly wage increase, an eight instead of a nine-hour work-day, and a 10-cent instead of a nickel

Sheriff Wilcox Takes Leading Role in Excitement Over Report 'Saucer' Found

U. S. Lend-Lease To Britain Looms As Needed by Fall

London, July 9, (AP) — Parliament had a hint from the government today, only three days prior to the Paris economic conference, that renewal of United States lend-lease before fall might be necessary to save Britain from unproductive poverty.

That worried look on the face of Sheriff George Wilcox, in the picture above, comes from having been cast, more suddenly than he liked, into the role of leading man in the world comedy which developed over the purported finding of a flying saucer at the Foster ranch, in the Corona community, northwest of Roswell.

Wilcox is shown here talking to a high English official who told him, "we are just as much interested in your disks as you are," and attempted to secure more information from the officer than had been revealed through Associated Press services a couple of hours earlier.

Arrest 2,000 In Athens in Commie Plot

Revolution Was Set to Be Pulled Off Thursday

Athens, July 9, (AP) — The Greek government announced that more than 2,000 persons were arrested in the Athens area early today in raids aimed at stamping out a Communist plot to stage a revolution and spread civil war throughout the country.

Minister of Public Order Napoleon Zervas said the zero hour for the Communist stroke was to have been around 1 a. m. tomorrow, when attacks were to have been staged simultaneously in all parts of Greece, bringing the present mountain guerilla warfare into urban centers.

Between 3,000 and 4,000 police, gendarmes and soldiers staged the lightning raids before dawn this morning, Zervas said. He added that many important Communists already had fled and either were hiding in Athens or in the mountains.

Most of those arrested, he said, will be taken to islands near Athens, while the investigation continues.

The transport already has begun. Some ringleaders, Zervas added, will remain in Athens to await hearings. Those not implicated in the plot will be released and others probably will be exiled, officials said.

A leftist leader who escaped arrest in the first raids declared "They're making a clean sweep."

—0—

Attorney to Force Closing up of Ruidoso Clubrooms

Las Cruces, July 9, (AP) — Back from a two-week vacation, District Attorney W. T. Scoggin, Jr. today announced injunction papers are being drawn up to force closing of clubrooms at Ruidoso

Send First Roswell Wire Ph

Local Weatherman Believes Disks to Be Bureau Devices

Weatherman L. J. Guthrie, of the Roswell bureau of the United States weather service, today was disposed to agree with army officials that the so-called disk found on the Foster ranch, northwest of Roswell by W. W. Brazel, and recovered by the army air forces at RAAF, was one belonging to the weather service.

The weather service has been

RECORD PHONES
Business Office 2288
News Department 2287

6c PER COPY

ellSaucer

cord Office

Ramey Says Excitement Is Not Justified

General Ramey Says Disk Is Weather Balloon

Tehran, July 9. ?—The flying saucer fever spread to Iran today.

Press reports from Zabool, Shoosf and Sarbisheh near the Afghan frontier said residents there had observed strange "starlike bodies" in the sky which exploded loudly, leaving a cloud of smoke.

The newspaper Mehri Iran said the objects apparently had something to do with a secret weapon, which it dubbed "V-20."

Fort Worth, Texas, July 9. 4?.— An examination by the army revealed last night that mysterious objects found on a lonely New Mexico ranch was a harmless high-altitude weather balloon—not a grounded flying disk.

Excitement was high until Brig. Gen. Roger M. Ramey, commander of the Eighth air forces with headquarters here cleared up the mystery.

The bundle of tinfoil, broken wood beams and rubber remnants of a balloon were sent here yesterday by army air transport in the wake of reports that it was a flying disk.

But the general said the objects were the crushed remains of a ray wind target used to determine the direction and velocity of winds at high altitudes.

Warrant Officer Irving Newton, forecaster at the army air forces weather station here, said, "we use them because they go much higher than the eye can see."

The weather balloon was found several days ago near the center of New Mexico by Rancher W. W. Brasel. He said he didn't think much about it until he went into Corona, N. M., last Saturday and heard the flying disk reports.

He returned to his ranch 85 miles northwest of Roswell, and recovered the wreckage of the balloon, which he had placed under some brush.

Then Brasel hurried back to Roswell, where he reported his find

Romania Rejects Bid to Take Part In Economic Meet

Paris, July 9 (AP)—Romania rejected today the British-French invitation to a Paris conference on the Marshall aid-to-Europe proposal, and became the second nation in the Russian sphere to decline the bid. Bulgaria's rejection came last night.

The Romanian cabinet issued a communique rejecting the invitation.

The newspaper's editorial column inside was headed 'And now what is it?' It ran:

With the telephone ringing, excited voices shouting into newsroom personnel ears pouring out eager questions which were unanswerable, it was discovered shortly after publication time of the Record *yesterday afternoon that curiosity over reports from 44 states of the Union that silver discs had been seen had crystallised into belief.*

The Record *had no more than hit the street until the telephone barrage began, with questioners checking up on what they had just read, doubtful of their own eyes.*

But the story stood, just as all amazing things stand in these days of wonderful feats and curious performances.

What the disc is is another matter. The Army isn't telling its secrets yet, from all appearances when this was written. Maybe it's a fluke, and maybe it isn't. Anyone's guess is pretty good at the moment.

Maybe the thing is still a hoax, as has been the belief of most folks from the start. But, SOMETHING has been found.

Thereafter the story of a flying saucer crash at Roswell died. At least, as far as the outside world was concerned. Local people who had lived through those days in July continued to talk about it. Some had personal experiences that indicated to them that the truth was not exactly as the USAAF had painted it. But these were good, patriotic US citizens and the world was a dangerous place. If the USAAF wanted the thing hushed up, then that was just fine.

It would be many years before the story was reborn.

◀ The front page of the *Roswell Daily Record* from 9 July 1947, carrying the explanation that effectively killed the Roswell story for decades.

2

Roswell
Reborn

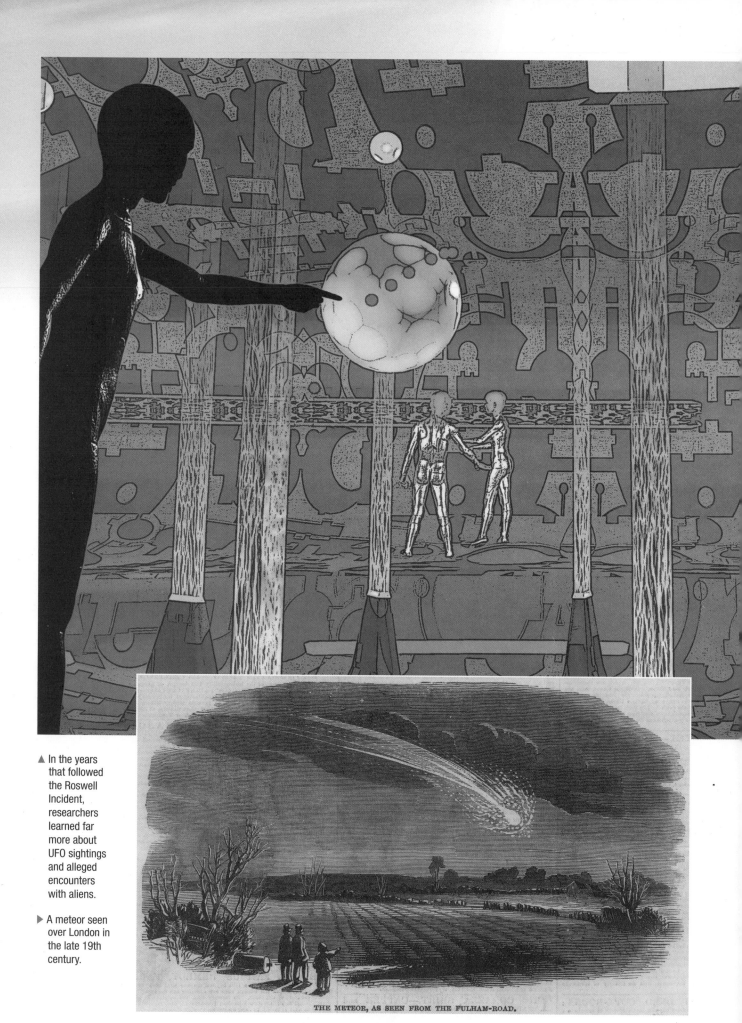

▲ In the years that followed the Roswell Incident, researchers learned far more about UFO sightings and alleged encounters with aliens.

▶ A meteor seen over London in the late 19th century.

THE METEOR, AS SEEN FROM THE FULHAM-ROAD.

saucers' or 'flying disks' had by the 1950s become more generally known as UFOs. The term originated with the USAAF which had wanted to use a phrase when dealing with sightings of these mysterious craft that did not imply a belief in the fact that they actually existed at all. UFO stands for Unidentified Flying Object, and accurately describes the official status of any object seen in the sky that cannot be readily identified as something mundane such as an aircraft or a meteor.

The official views of the USAAF, US government and most governments around the world had become firmly entrenched by 1978, and remain unchanged today. UFOs are exactly that, they are unidentified objects. Any sighting that cannot be readily identified is classed as 'unidentified'. The official line is that all these objects could be identified as something ordinary if only a bit more information had been obtained by the witness, or if the witness had been familiar with the less often seen types of aircraft or natural aerial phenomena.

PROJECT SIGN

For a while the USAAF, RAF and other defence organizations had taken an active interest in UFOs, worried that they might be some form of foreign secret weapon. In September 1947 the USAAF had set up Project Sign to analyze the reports of flying saucers. The staff working on Project Sign were seconded from the Air Technical Intelligence Center at Wright Air Field. They found themselves deluged with hundreds of reports, only some of which could be studied in any detail. They decided to concentrate on reports made by people such as military officers or civil airline pilots, who could be considered to be familiar with aircraft and inherently trustworthy.

The Project Sign staff were instructed to come up with conclusions and recommendations as quickly as possible. In 1948 they

BY 1978 THE STUDY of UFOs had moved on considerably since the hectic days of July 1947 when Roswell was temporarily gripped by flying saucer fever. A lot more had been learned about the mysterious flying objects, and about the humanoids that were reported to emerge from them when they landed. While the vast mass of information about UFOs could – and indeed has – filled numerous volumes, that which is relevant to the Roswell case can be summarized fairly quickly.

What in 1947 had been called 'flying

produced a highly classified document entitled 'The Estimate of the Situation', which has since entered UFO legend. The report concluded that the USA was being visited by mechanical craft with flying abilities far in advance of anything that the USAAF was capable of putting into the air. It went on to analyze what was then known of Soviet and other foreign aircraft, and concluded that the flying disks were also far in advance of any known or suggested aircraft of any nation on earth. The conclusion drawn from this was that the flying saucers were almost certainly spaceships from another planet.

'The Estimate of the Situation' was delivered to none other than General Hoyt Vandenberg, the second-in-command of the USAAF, who had handled the Roswell Incident from the Pentagon. By all accounts, he erupted into a towering rage when he first read the report. When he had calmed down, Vandenberg issued a terse and pointed memo that dismissed the report's conclusions on the

grounds that there was not enough evidence to come to any conclusion at all. He then ordered that all copies of the report be destroyed. So far as is known his orders were carried out and no copy of 'The Estimate of the Situation' has ever seen the light of day.

PROJECT GRUDGE

Project Sign was then wound up and replaced by Project Grudge, which ran from 11 February 1949 to December the same year. The staff working on Grudge were given instructions that they were to find a rational explanation for every sighting of a UFO reported to them. They recruited several experts in aircraft and aerial phenomena to help them. Among these was an astronomer named J. Allen Hynek. He was sent eyewitness reports and asked if they could be explained away as meteors, shooting stars, normal stars seen in odd atmospheric conditions and the like. At this time Hynek believed that all UFO reports were misidentified mundane objects and readily complied, marking reports as either 'explained' in astronomical terms or as 'unexplained' whereupon he expected them to be passed on to other experts to see if they could interpret them.

The staff working on Project Grudge went to enormous lengths to fulfil their allotted task of explaining away each and every sighting. Notoriously when faced with a sighting that could not be explained, they sought to undermine and smear the person who had made the report so that they could credibly say the sighting was an hallucination or deliberate fraud. Grudge ended with a declaration that there was no such thing as a flying saucer from outer space, only objects as yet unidentified.

PROJECT BLUE BOOK

In March 1952, the USAF set up a new study group called Project Blue Book, which was headed by a lowly captain, indicating that the USAAF gave it a low priority. It had few staff, most of them part-time, and almost no resources beyond an office, a few phone lines and virtually unlimited file storage space. The task of Project Blue Book was mostly to collect and file UFO reports. Only if the media made a fuss were Blue Book staff to investigate the sighting. Then, as with Grudge, the staff were instructed to find a conventional explanation if at all possible. In 1969 Blue Book concluded that whatever UFOs were, they were no threat to the air defence of the USA and therefore no business of the USAAF. The project was shut down.

Meanwhile, many people interested in the UFO phenomenon had become increasingly frustrated by the official dismissals of evidence. Throughout the 1950s and 1960s a growing band of amateurs collated sightings reports and did their best to investigate the better quality events. Their efforts ran parallel to sensationalist science fiction novels and

films as well as some highly dubious claims by people who said that they had met and talked to aliens – most of whom were very human – who had emerged from landed saucers.

In the early 1960s the study of UFOs moved out of the fringes in which it had languished as a number of investigators and research groups began publishing books that adopted a serious and in many cases rigorous methodology. The growing respectability of UFO research, at least among the public, was helped by some high-profile cases involving clear sightings by witnesses who could not be written off as cranks.

PERSUASIVE EVIDENCE

In 1961 Betty and Barney Hill, an eminently respectable couple, were apparently abducted from their car late at night by diminutive aliens that took them on board a UFO for

▼ The famous Project Blue Book was commissioned by the USAAF in a clear policy decision to explain UFO sightings in conventional terms.

FLYING SAUCERS:

AN ANALYSIS OF THE
AIR FORCE
PROJECT BLUE BOOK
SPECIAL REPORT No. 14

INCLUDING

THE C.I.A. AND THE SAUCERS

FIFTH EDITION
DECEMBER, 1976

PREPARED BY
DR. LEON DAVIDSON

▲ An artwork of the Hill Case, one of the first encounters to include a temporary abduction of the human witnesses.

medical experimentation. In April 1964 a New Mexico policeman named Lonnie Zamora saw a UFO land in the desert outside Socorro. He saw two humanoids about 4 ft (1.2 m) tall which, on becoming aware that Zamora was approaching, got back in to the UFO and flew off. These were but the tip of an iceberg that included hundreds of credible reports.

A few serious scientists began to change their minds. Among these was J. Allen Hynek. During the 1960s Hynek became increasingly disillusioned with Project Blue Book, to which he had been transferred from Project Grudge. He was beginning to realize that not all reports could be dismissed as easily as he had thought. Hynek began investigating a few cases on his own and by the later 1960s had become convinced that there was some underlying reality to the UFO sightings that needed to be investigated.

In 1972 Hynek announced his change of mind in spectacular fashion when he published *The UFO Experience*. In this book, he set out several of the cases that he had dealt with and, while avoiding endorsing any particular explanation, made it clear that he thought that UFOs were real, as were the humanoids seen emerging from them. Crucially, the book included a new classification system for UFO sightings that quickly caught on. This categorized distant sightings that could not be explained, but which had little detail. Then there were what Hynek termed 'close encounters'. A close encounter of the first kind involved a witness seeing a UFO at such close quarters that it could not possibly be confused with anything mundane. A close encounter of the second kind involved a witness seeing the UFO have physical effects on its surroundings, such as singeing plant material or leaving marks where it landed. A close encounter of the third kind occurred when the witness saw apparently living crew emerge from the UFO.

By this date it was widely accepted among

▲ Police officer Lonnie Zamora who sighted a landed UFO and its crew in New Mexico in 1964.

Hynek was beginning to realize that not all reports could be dismissed as easily as he had thought.

could not be simply written off as being a sighting of something mundane under unusual circumstances, as many views of more distant objects could. He was prepared to accept that some UFOs were mechanical craft and that some of the humanoids sighted did come out of UFOs and were a reality. Cautiously, however, he was not prepared to go much further – at least in public. His involvement with Roswell would change all that.

UNEARTHING A WITNESS

In 1978 Friedman travelled to Baton Rouge, Louisiana, to take part in a television show that was discussing the subject of UFOs and aliens. As anyone who has done TV work will know there is an inordinate amount of waiting around while lights, cameras and other details are sorted out. Friedman was accordingly filling in time chatting to the technical crew at the studio when one of them mentioned that there was a retired USAAF man living over at Houna, Louisiana, who claimed to have seen a crashed UFO during his time with the USAAF. Friedman had heard such rumours before, but none of the stories had been backed up by any evidence.

This time it seemed different. The crewman knew the man in question well and was willing to vouch for him. The retired USAAF man in question was identified as Jesse Marcel, an officer with a distinguished record both during wartime and peace. With a potential witness, this story promised to be something different. Friedman found Marcel's name in a phone book and called him.

This first interview between Friedman and Marcel was rather brief, but it furnished Friedman with the basics of Marcel's version of events. Over the years that followed, Marcel would be interviewed dozens of times by other researchers and for television shows about Roswell. There were small discrepancies of detail between the different versions (that

▲ Jesse Marcel photographed after his retirement from the USAF. It was Marcel who first claimed that the wreckage he handled could not have come from a terrestrial aircraft.

UFO researchers and those who took the concept seriously that the objects were alien spacecraft bringing intelligent beings to Earth. The purpose of the visits was a matter of controversy. Some thought the aliens were hostile, others that they were benevolent. Abductions were, by 1978, being reported more frequently but had not as yet achieved the dominance in the field that they would some twenty years later.

At this time there was only one other professional scientist who was willing to declare publicly his belief that UFOs were a real phenomena that were worth investigating. That was Stanton Friedman. It was Friedman who would unearth the Roswell Incident and launch the first of several investigations into the events of 1947.

Friedman spent most of his working life as a nuclear physicist, working for companies such as General Electric and General Motors. In 1978, his attitude was that a large number of UFO sightings were of such high quality and described the objects in such detail that they we will come to later) and sceptics have seized on these to try to discredit Marcel as a witness.

In truth, however, the discrepancies in Marcel's testimony at different times merely highlight one of the key problems regarding the entire Roswell Incident. The new, more methodical breed of UFO investigators who were active in the 1970s and 1980s did not get to hear about the events of July 1947 until more than thirty years after the event. Many of the people who had been involved at the time had died; others were getting on in years.

A good number of those who had witnessed the events first-hand and who were still alive had been involved only on the periphery of the action. The things they had seen and experienced had struck them as odd and unusual – and inconsistent with the official version of events given out by the USAAF – but they had not been earth-shattering. After thirty years it was inevitable that memories might be rather hazy and at times confused. Even witnesses who were acting in good faith might muddle events, confuse the order in which things happened or misremember the other people involved. There would be numerous frustrations ahead for Friedman and the others who investigated Roswell.

SUBJECTIVE MEMORIES

Another common problem with eyewitness testimony, especially when it is given a few years after the events described, is a discrepancy between what the witness describes seeing and how he or she interprets it. Very often the interpretation is coloured by the circumstances in which the events took place. As the years pass the interpretation of what has been seen can become confused with what was actually seen. Indeed, it can become firmly entrenched in the mind of the witness so that, when asked about the event, the witness claims in all good faith to have seen something that he or she did not.

▲ Stanton Friedman was the first UFO researcher to take the Roswell Incident seriously, interviewing witnesses and putting together a tentative sequence of events.

It is probably best to illustrate this problem using an example that is unrelated to either Roswell or UFOs in general. A person might meet an old friend of his in a bar or pub and stop to chat for a while. That friend might be holding in his hand a drink consisting of a clear, bubbly liquid in a tall glass together with ice and lemon. Knowing his friend likes gin and tonic, the man may assume that the drink in the glass is a gin and tonic, though it may just as easily be a lemonade or mineral water.

If some days later the man is asked when he last saw his friend, he might reply that it was in a bar and that his friend was having a gin and tonic, because that is how he interpreted what he saw. With most witnesses it is usual for this tendency to become more entrenched over time. It would not be more than a month or two before the witness was convinced that his friend had been drinking gin and tonic and might even go so far as to deny that he had been drinking lemonade.

When reading witness statements it is, therefore, crucial to try to distinguish between what a witness describes seeing and how they interpret what they were seeing. It is not always easy and in reading some witness statements relating to the Roswell Incident it can be very difficult indeed. Such are the problems which may be encountered when dealing with honest, dependable witnesses who are acting in good faith.

Of course, not all witnesses would turn out to be acting in good faith. As the years rolled by and Roswell became increasingly famous, even iconic, it attracted a number of people who claimed to have seen things and to have been involved in the incident. Some of these witnesses are accepted by most researchers as genuine. They are people who have kept quiet for decades either because they thought it was the right thing to do after military personnel asked them to remain silent, or because they have feared ridicule.

Other witnesses who have come forward have more dubious stories to tell. Some researchers accept what they have to say at face value while others discount them as being either liars or mistaken. There are all sorts of reasons why a person might invent testimony about the Roswell Incident. An obvious starter is a desire for fame and money. Witnesses who are able to reveal a key fact can expect to have their names included in books and magazine articles. And they can command relatively high fees for appearing on documentary programmes. There may also be other reasons. Some people can become confused between what genuinely happened to them and what they have seen in movies. They may believe what they say is true even when it is not. And some people simply have a mischievous sense of humour that spurs them on to hoodwink the public and serious researchers.

Not all witnesses fit neatly into one or other category. As we shall see, some witnesses have altered their stories over the years as they have 'suddenly remembered' things

that they had previously forgotten. More than one observer when first interviewed has relayed an interesting but not particularly exciting account. When interviewed again some years later, however, they have produced an astonishing story of truly amazing content.

Trying to sort out one type of witness from another has proved to be very difficult. Some witnesses are accepted as genuine by one researcher, but rejected as spurious by another. The tale told by a witness early in the investigation may be accepted by all, but his more thrilling version of events given later will be rejected as a fiction designed to increase fees received for TV appearances.

As we shall see, the research into the Roswell Incident has been plagued by dis-

agreements between researchers – and that is before the outright scorn of sceptics is taken into account.

MARCEL'S TESTIMONY

The essentials of Marcel's story have, however, remained consistent throughout. In his very first conversation with Friedman, Marcel related his version of the events that took place. In general his account tallied with the official version, but there were two important differences. The first was that the material that he collected from the Foster Ranch had some very strange properties indeed. The thin metallic sheets were as light as paper but were incredibly strong. They could not be bent

▲ A magazine illustration from the 1940s showing ranchers finding mysterious crashed debris. In this case the debris is clearly identified as being a test aircraft flown by the USAF.

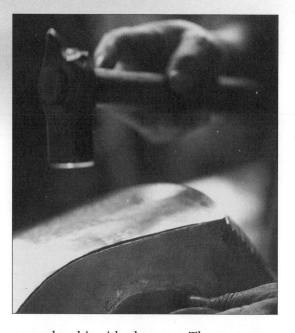

▶ Witnesses claimed that the wreckage found at Roswell was resistant to hammer blows.

even when hit with a hammer. The struts were also immensely tough but very light. Other witnesses who handled the material would make similar claims that we shall study in depth later.

The second claim made by Marcel was that the wreckage shown to reporters at Fort Worth was not the same as the debris he had brought in from Roswell. Marcel claimed that the original debris had been removed and

> **Marcel had made attempts to find out what had happened at Roswell in his absence. All his inquiries were blocked or answered by the statement that the whole affair was to be forgotten.**

switched for what was, as Ramey had claimed it to be, the wreckage of a balloon. According to Marcel, Ramey had at first welcomed Marcel and his boxes of debris. Later he had become brusque to the point of rudeness. Ramey had informed Marcel that he was taking over possession of and responsibility for the material and that the whole business

had to be hushed up. There then followed the switch of material and the meeting with the reporters. Marcel had then been ordered back to Roswell.

When he returned to his office, Marcel had made attempts to find out the reasons for the change of heart and to discover what had happened at Roswell in his absence. All his inquiries were blocked or answered by the statement that the whole affair was to be forgotten as quickly and completely as possible. At the time Marcel had assumed that this secrecy was to be a purely temporary measure while the USAAF sorted the affair out. However, as the months and then years rolled by it became evident that the USAAF was not going to make any public statement at all. Marcel grew disillusioned, but as a career officer he got on with his job and pushed the events at Roswell to the back of his mind. After he retired Marcel felt able to speak out and had raised the subject a few times. It was not until he met Friedman that he found anyone willing to take him seriously.

Unfortunately for Friedman, Marcel had lost his records and mementos of his military service. Although he could recall that the alleged flying saucer crash had occurred in a summer during his service at Roswell, he could not recall the year.

After that first interview with Marcel, Friedman was of the opinion that he had unearthed a very interesting story that would be worth investigating. However, he knew from bitter experience that without a firm date to use as a starting point, the research involved would be almost impossible.

Nevertheless, on his return to his office, Friedman spent some time trawling through his copious notes and files on UFO reports. He thought he recalled having come across a tale linked to a UFO crash in New Mexico before. After some time he found it.

It was a note from Lydia Sleppy who, in the late 1940s, had been working on administrative duties at KOAT, a radio station in Albuquerque, New Mexico. She had told Friedman about an odd incident that had occurred one summer afternoon in the late 1940s. Sleppy had answered the newsroom phone and found herself talking to Johnny McBoyle, a reporter for KOAT's sister station in Roswell, KSWS. McBoyle had sounded very excited. He told Sleppy to get the teletype machine out and get ready to send out a news report that he was going to dictate to her over the phone.

As closely as Sleppy had been able to remember McBoyle's message after a passage of twenty odd years, she quoted him as having said:

Lydia, get ready for a scoop. We want this to go on the wire right away. A flying saucer has crashed here near Roswell. I've been there and seen it. It's like a big, crumpled dishpan. Some rancher has hauled it under a cattle shelter. The Army is there and they are going to pick it up. The whole area is now closed off. And get this – they are saying something about little men on board.

Sleppy was frantically busy typing McBoyle's words into the teletype, but at that point the line went dead. Although unusual, this was not unheard of. KOAT was not a major station and sometimes other newsfeeds took priority. Sleppy told McBoyle the line was down and that he would have to wait. McBoyle then seemed to be having a conversation with somebody at his end of the line. It sounded a rather fraught affair, but Sleppy did not catch the details.

The teletype then sprang into life, but before she could ask McBoyle to start dictating again an incoming message marked 'high priority' came through. According to Sleppy it read along the lines of: 'Attention Albuquerque. Do not transmit. Repeat, do not transmit this message. Stop communica-

tion immediately'. Sleppy could not recall precisely, but thought it had come from the FBI or police. She knew that with so many military secrets in the region they did sometimes monitor phone lines and other communications.

Sleppy told McBoyle about the message and asked him what she should do. There was a pause, again while he seemed to be talking to somebody else. Then McBoyle told Sleppy to forget all about it, to pretend she had never heard anything. She did, in fact, tell the owner of KOAT, Merle Tucker, when he returned to the office a short time later. Tucker said he would look into it, but Sleppy heard no more about it. She assumed it was some military matter that was best left alone. She did not discuss it until years later when she talked to Friedman.

ARCHIVE INVESTIGATION

Friedman now had two first-hand stories about a UFO crash in New Mexico in the late 1940s, but still no firm date. He contacted another UFO researcher, William Moore, for help. Moore had his own records that tied in with the stories of Marcel and Sleppy. Among Moore's records were complete file copies of the journal *Flying Saucer Review*. This was

'Attention Albuquerque. Do not transmit. Repeat, do not transmit this message. Stop communication immediately.'

one of the more serious UFO magazines running at the time. It had begun publication in 1955 and featured only reports that had been subjected to some sort of research and verification, as well as theories and ideas put together by those with some scientific background. Moore looked up a story that he recalled about a UFO crash in New Mexico. It

Roswell Reborn

The discovery by researchers of this headline in the *Roswell Daily Record* of 8 July 1947 allowed them to pinpoint the date of the Roswell Incident. Later there would be disputes about the exact timing of events.

was an early piece written by Hughie Green after his break into television entertainment. This time there was a date. Green knew that his journey through New Mexico had taken place on 8 July 1947 and that the UFO crash was reported to have taken place at Roswell.

Armed with this date and firm location, Moore went to search the archive files of newspapers from New Mexico. Within a very short time he turned up the story in the *Roswell Daily Record* that announced a saucer had crashed and been recovered by the USAAF, together with the story the next day that repeated the USAAF claim that the saucer was only a weather balloon.

Moore and Friedman now had definite

contemporary evidence that confirmed the outline of Marcel's story, and which also chimed with Sleppy's. A flying saucer was reported to have crashed but the USAAF had subsequently scotched the story by saying it was only a weather balloon. According to Marcel the first part of the story had been true, but the second report had been a fabrication put out by the USAAF to hush up the story. Sleppy's story also indicated that an initial report had been quickly followed by an official denial.

The contemporary newspaper reports unearthed by Moore included numerous names of people said to be involved in the initial discovery of the crashed saucer. Among

these were the rancher Mac Brazel, Sheriff George Wilcox, the Roswell air base press officer Walter Haut, and Jesse Marcel. They also gave the names of the men involved with disseminating the story about the weather balloon, including General Ramey and Warrant Officer Newton. Moore and Friedman decided that this was enough to warrant a proper investigation, so they set about finding the men named. They also trav-

elled to Roswell to try to find people who had been living in the area in 1947 and remembered anything about the events that took place.

By 1980, Moore and Friedman believed that they had unearthed enough evidence to prove that the object that had crashed was not a weather balloon. They also felt that the evidence pointed towards the fact that the crashed object was a flying machine of incred-

▲ William Moore (right) speaking at a conference organized by MUFON. It was the book co-authored by Moore that brought the Roswell Incident to the attention of the world.

ibly advanced and sophisticated design, and that it was probably an alien spaceship. They then contacted Charles Berlitz, a writer with huge experience of producing popular books and articles on paranormal subjects and unsolved mysteries. Berlitz was adept at marshalling evidence of the most bizarre events into a rational format and explaining the often esoteric concepts in everyday language.

The result of this collaboration was the book *The Roswell Incident*, which was published in 1980. The authors were given as Berlitz and Moore, with Friedman credited as a researcher. The book was only a modest success when first published, though as the Roswell story became better known it was reprinted.

What the book did achieve was to launch the Roswell story into the forefront of UFO research. The allegation that a UFO had crashed at Roswell and been impounded by the USAAF spread rapidly through the community of those interested in UFOs. Slowly, statements by witnesses that corroborated the story were gathered together. Some of these witnesses related tales of a UFO or of alien bodies being held amid conditions of great security by the USAAF or the US government. Others told of coming across pieces of material or technology that were so advanced as to seem to be of alien origin. Again these objects were usually said to be in the possession of the USAAF or US government.

Meanwhile, Friedman, Moore and teams working with them continued to track down people who had been in Roswell in July 1947 to ask them for their memories. One of the most productive contacts proved to be the former press officer, Walter Haut. Unlike Marcel, he had kept a quantity of papers, photos and other memorabilia of his time in the USAAF, much of which related to Roswell. He was able to provide researchers with dozens of names of people who had been on site at the crucial time.

▲ UFO researcher Donald Schmitt spent a great deal of time in the 1980s seeking out witnesses and analyzing statements.

APPEAL FOR WITNESSES

Then in 1989, the Roswell story was featured in an episode of the hugely popular TV series *Unsolved Mysteries*. The show ended with an appeal for anyone who knew anything or who had been around Roswell in July 1947 to call a phone number that was given on-screen. This produced a large number of new witnesses, though they were judged by researchers to be of varying reliability.

By 1991, UFO researchers Kevin Randle and Donald Schmitt felt that they had gathered enough new evidence to warrant the writing of an entirely new book about Roswell. This was entitled *UFO Crash at Roswell* and sold very well indeed. The new offering generally followed the main themes of the earlier book, but included much more in the way of eyewitness testimony to back up the claims. A few details of the story and timeline were altered to fit the new evidence, but otherwise it was mostly an expansion of the first book.

The following year, Stanton Friedman produced his own book on the subject. The book had been eagerly awaited by those in the UFO community who had known of his involvement in the investigation from the start. The book was entitled *Crash at Corona*, since the Foster Ranch and alleged site of the crash was actually closer to Corona than to Roswell.

In large part, Friedman's book concentrated on the contents of a collection of documents that are collectively known as 'Majestic 12'. These are controversial even among those researchers who believe that UFOs are alien spaceships and that the US government is covering up the truth. As we shall see when we study them in more detail, they purport to be official US government documents dating to 1952 that prove that the USAAF has possession of a crashed alien spaceship. Although they caused a great stir at the time they first emerged in the mid-1980s, most researchers now believe that they are forgeries.

The rest of the book was largely devoted to the new accounts given by the witnesses who had come forward after the 1989 television show. In this work Friedman seemed more willing to believe these witnesses than had Randle and Schmitt in their 1991 book. The evidence added some exciting, not to say sensational details, but it was not all accepted uncritically by other researchers. Nevertheless, it is these accounts that have been taken up by screenwriters for movies and TV. The events at Roswell have featured in numerous fictional shows, and it is generally the more sensational claims that have made it on to the screen.

In 1994, Randle and Schmitt responded to Friedman's book with a new one of their own entitled *The Truth about the UFO Crash at Roswell*. This book itself included some new

and sensational witness claims, while ignoring or denouncing some of those included by Friedman. Interestingly, it put forward a revised timeline for the alleged UFO crash and subsequent events. It also changed some of the locations where events were said to have occurred.

Thereafter the UFO research community, together with the books and articles that it produces, has been divided. Some follow the revised Randle-Schmitt timeline and broadly accept their witnesses as genuine. Others remain faithful to the original timeline as propounded by Berlitz and Moore, and prefer to believe the witnesses highlighted by Friedman. There have been attempts to rec-

> **The events at Roswell have featured in numerous fictional shows, and it is generally the more sensational claims that have made it on to the screen.**

oncile the two versions of the story, but these have always foundered.

Then a dramatic new turn came in July 1994. Steven Schiff, the New Mexico Congressman whose constituency covered Roswell, had become interested in the case, but was frustrated by what he felt to be offhand and casual dismissals from the United States Air Force (USAF) whenever he asked for information. Feeling that a Congressman acting on behalf of the public should be able to expect more serious responses, Schiff had turned to the General Accounting Office (GAO) of the US government.

OFFICIAL REPORTS

The GAO insisted that the USAF carry out a thorough investigation into events at Roswell, and also contacted other government agencies on the subject. The result was two reports, one from the USAF and one from the GAO, which were broadly similar. These both concluded that there had been a crash at Roswell in July 1947 and that the USAAF had deliberately misled the public and covered up the truth by spreading a false story that the object that had crashed was only a weather balloon. In fact, the reports stated, the object had been a balloon. But it had not been a simple weather balloon but a top secret device

> **The reports admitted that vast amounts of official documentation relating to Roswell and the 509th Bomber Group for 1947 had simply vanished.**

launched as part of Project Mogul – a highly classified programme that was spying on the Soviet attempts to build an atomic bomb.

While sceptics found the reports convincing and claimed they had undermined the Roswell story, others were not so sure. They pointed out that they ignored much of the evidence and that their own chronology of events was self-contradictory. Above all, the reports admitted that vast amounts of official documentation relating to Roswell and the 509th Bomber Group for 1947 had simply vanished. The files were not where they should be and there was no indication as to where they had gone, why they had gone or even who had ordered their removal.

In 1995 Kevin Randle went into print with a book entitled *Roswell UFO Crash Update*. It was largely a demolition of the official USAF and GAO reports, and an update on several

▶ A photograph of a Project Mogul balloon. The balloon in this photo is only partially inflated; it would only inflate fully as it reached higher altitudes where the air pressure was much lower.

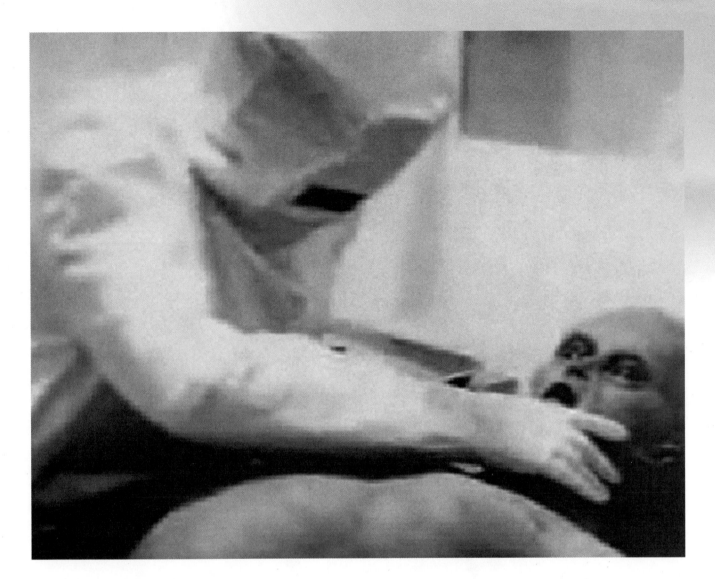

minor issues relating to witnesses and their statements.

In 1995 another dramatic new turn emerged when what was to become known as the 'Alien Autopsy Footage' was revealed by film producer Ray Santilli. Santilli claimed that the footage had been shot in 1947 and was of an autopsy carried out on an alien retrieved from the Roswell crash. He said that he had obtained it from a former USAAF cameraman who had been involved in filming all sorts of secret projects – including atomic bomb tests – and who had managed to secrete this particular can of film. It was now being offered for sale by the anonymous cameraman who wanted some money for undisclosed reasons, but presumably to fund his retirement.

The Alien Autopsy Footage proved to be highly controversial. It did, indeed, seem to show a few minutes of an autopsy being carried out on a humanoid figure that resembled the descriptions given by those who claimed to have seen the alien bodies alleged to have been recovered at Roswell. However, special effects specialists were of the opinion that it could have been easily faked, although they put the price tag for such a fake at around $200,000. There were also problems relating to the age of the film itself and the reality of the cameraman alleged to have been holding the film can for the past fifty years. In 2006, Santilli finally admitted that the footage was not genuine, but he maintained that he was as much a victim of the fraud as anyone else.

By 2009, the story of the Roswell Incident seems to have come full circle. The original witnesses are dying off, and it seems highly unlikely that any new observers of the original events are going to come forward. It is time to review the evidence and try to put together the story, taking into account the contradictions between the stories told by different witnesses and documents.

▲ A still from the notorious 'alien autopsy' movie, now generally recognized as being a fake.

3
The Crash

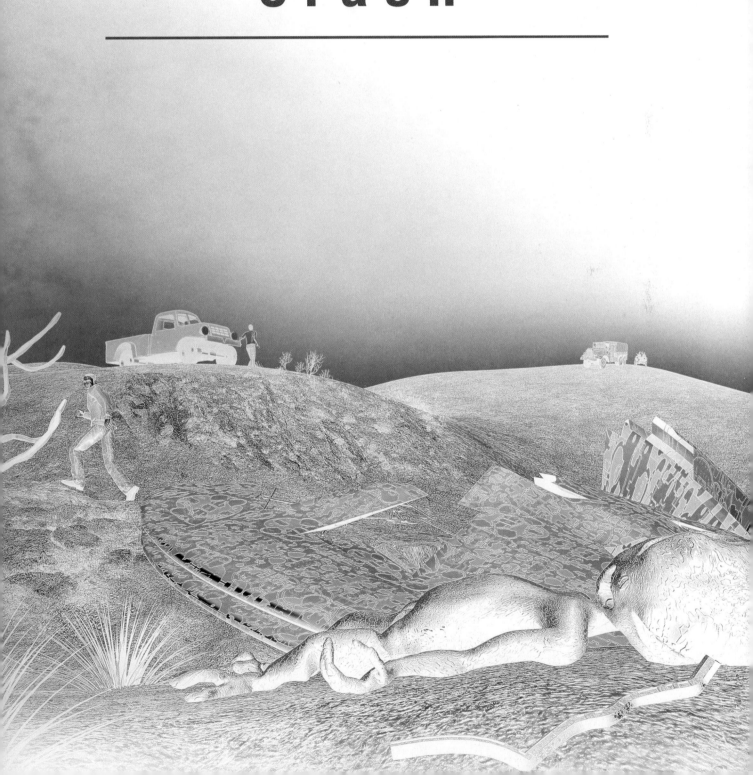

A few days before the Roswell Incident hit the headlines, Dan Wilmot sighted a UFO streaking through the skies over Roswell.

THOSE INVESTIGATING the crash at Roswell have, over the years, sought to discover just exactly what it was that crashed near the town, when it crashed and what happened to it afterwards. In trying to piece this train of events together, researchers have had to amalgamate evidence from a variety of sources, some of them more reliable than others. To read some reconstructions of the events of July 1947 it would seem that the sequence has been firmly established, but this is still very far from being the case.

The first piece of information that needs to be established is exactly when the crash took place – for even the sceptics are agreed that something crashed near Roswell. The starting point for most researchers on this has been the contemporary releases that went out over the AP wire and the newspaper accounts based on them.

The AP wire account and the first *Roswell Daily Record* story both went out on Tuesday 8 July 1947. These base their information quite clearly on what Mac Brazel told Sheriff Wilcox when he first reported his discovery and subsequently repeated to the USAAF officers who interviewed him – initially Major Jesse Marcel.

These variously stated that the crash had happened 'sometime last week' or 'a few days ago'. This would place the date sometime between Monday 30 June and Sunday 6 July. There is nothing in the contemporary accounts to fix the date any more clearly.

Bill Brazel, when asked about his father's actions after finding the debris on his ranch, gave a more detailed timeline. According to Bill, Mac had spotted the debris in a pasture the day after a storm, but at first had not gone over to inspect it as he was busy with ranch jobs. But then 'after a day or so' he went for a closer look and realized that the debris was

something very out of the ordinary. 'That night', Mac had gone over to the Proctors' house to discuss the finds with Floyd Proctor. The next evening he had gone to Corona to talk to his brother-in-law, Hollis Wilson, and a friend. These two men advised Mac to report his finds to the authorities, and so 'the next day' Mac drove into Roswell to see Sheriff Wilcox.

We know that Brazel reported his findings to Wilcox on 7 July, so counting back it is clear that Bill Brazel's account has his father taking a closer look at the debris on 5 July. The crash, according to Bill, had taken place 'a day or so' before that. Assuming that this means a maximum of three days, this would put the crash between 2 and 4 July.

When interviewed, the Proctors recalled Mac Brazel's visit clearly, and knew that it had happened just before the flying saucer story broke in the local newspaper. They could not, however, recall Brazel telling them any firm date for when the crash had taken place except that it had been a few days earlier and that Brazel had only just found the spare time to make the journey to the Proctors.

WILMOT SIGHTING

However, the contemporary accounts did include a few other clues. One of these was a newspaper report printed the day after the main story. This related to a report made by Dan Wilmot, who ran the Roswell hardware store. Having seen the story about Brazel and

> **According to Bill, Mac had spotted the debris in a pasture the day after a storm, but at first had not gone over to inspect it as he was busy with ranch jobs.**

his crashed flying saucer, Wilmot had contacted the paper to say that he had seen a flying saucer himself a few days earlier. Wilmot did give a firm date – 2 July.

Wilmot said that he and his wife were sitting on the front porch of their home on South Penn Street in Roswell enjoying the cool evening air. A few minutes before 10 pm, Mrs Wilmot heard a whooshing noise and saw a large object flying overhead. She pointed it out to her husband. Living close to a busy airfield, the Wilmots were accustomed to seeing different types of aircraft at all times of day and night and at all altitudes, but this was something different.

The mysterious craft was shaped 'like two inverted saucers faced mouth to mouth'. Just as odd, it looked as if it were emitting a dull glow from all over its surface – rather as if a frosted glass bowl had a low-powered light bulb inside it. Mr Wilmot stepped off the porch into his front yard to get a better view. The object was moving at a speed consistent with a normal military aircraft, but the appearance of the thing was so odd that it made a huge impression. The craft remained in sight for about 40 seconds before it vanished into the distance. It was heading

> **The object was moving at a speed consistent with a normal military aircraft, but the appearance of the thing was so odd that it made a huge impression.**

north-west on a course that would take it almost directly over the Foster Ranch where Brazel was to find his debris.

When the newspaper carried the Wilmot story, it described the hardware store owner as 'one of the most respected and reliable citi-

zens in town'. No research carried out since has indicated anything different. It is safe to suppose that the Wilmots did see a strange object passing overhead on the evening of 2 July.

Most early researchers into the Roswell Incident presumed that the Wilmot UFO was the same as that which crashed. This would mean that it continued on its path to the north-west, encountered some sort of difficulties over the Foster Ranch, and crashed. It is for this reason that most early books and articles on the subject fixed the date of the crash as on the night of 2 July.

A FIRM DATE?

This crash date of 2 July does fit in with both the newspaper and AP accounts, and with Bill Brazel's recollections of what his father had told him. However, it is not without its problems and has been challenged.

The first problem with the 2 July date emerges from the interview with Mac Brazel printed in the *Roswell Daily Record* on 9 July. This was the issue of the newspaper that carried on its front page the USAAF story about the crashed disk being only a weather balloon. The interview with Brazel was a secondary story. During the course of this interview, Brazel said that he had first spotted the debris on 14 June but had not bothered to investigate it properly until more recently.

This version has the virtue of being contemporary with events. It meshes neatly with the account given by the Proctors that Brazel had found the debris some days before he visited them. At a pinch it could match Bill Brazel's version that his father had acted quickly only after going to inspect the debris more closely.

On the other hand it contradicts Bill Brazel's memory that his father had spotted the debris only 'a day or so' beforehand, and the Proctors seemed to think that this was about right but were not so definite on the subject. It is also at odds with the AP and newspaper reports that the debris was found 'a few days ago' or 'sometime last week' – unless they were referring to the date on which Brazel inspected it more closely and not when he first saw it.

Some researchers have pointed to the fact that by the time he gave his interview to the newspaper giving the 14 June date, Brazel had been in military custody for some time. We will return to this issue when studying the USAAF cover-up of the Roswell Incident, but for now it is worth noting that most researchers have discounted Brazel's mention of 14 June as worthless. They have assumed that the military put pressure on Mac Brazel to give this date as it would fit more properly with their false claim of a weather balloon being involved than would a date in early July. This is possible, but there is no real evidence to back it up.

The issue of the crash date was further confused – or clarified depending on the researcher's point of view – by evidence that emerged in the 1980s after the growing fame of the Roswell Incident prompted other witnesses to come forward.

One of these witnesses was Jim Ragsdale who, in 1947, was a young man living in Carlsbad in southern New Mexico. On Friday 4 July he left home with a companion to go on a three-day camping trip in the desert north of Roswell. He has always been clear about the date and where he went. The identity of his companion and the nature of their relationship have been rather more vague. The person was certainly a young lady and seems to have been Ragsdale's girlfriend, but not the woman that he subsequently married. This might give Ragsdale some personal reasons for being a bit hazy about the woman's identity. In any case, she has never come forward to give her version of events and so is not strictly relevant to Ragsdale's testimony.

STORMY NIGHT

According to Ragsdale he and his companion drove through Roswell, then headed north on Highway 48 (now Pine Lodge Road) for a few miles before turning off to take to the desert roads. Once they were well into the desert, they pitched camp. It proved to be a tempes-

Most researchers have discounted Brazel's mention of 14 June as worthless.

tuous evening as a strong wind blew and electric storms lashed the desert with lightning and some rain. By around 11 pm the storms had passed and quiet returned. At around 11.30 pm a bright light flashed out from the sky. At first the campers thought it was lightning heralding a return of the storms, but it lasted too long for lightning so Ragsdale poked his head out of the tent to have a look. He saw a flying object heading towards him. He described the object as being incredibly bright and of a blue-white colour. He likened it to the light of an arc welder. The object flew rapidly on a diving course and hit the ground with a loud thump.

Ragsdale has always claimed to be reasonably certain of the location of the crash that he witnessed on 4 July 1947. This was because in the 1950s he was employed by the El Paso Natural Gas Company to survey a route for a gas pipeline and became very familiar with the area. His campsite was, he said, about 40 miles (65 km) north of Roswell and some 3 or 4 miles (5 or 6 km) west of the main road to the town of Vaughn.

Another witness who put the date of the crash on Friday 4 July was William Woody, though his evidence was not so clear. Woody said that he had been at his father's house a few miles north of Roswell one evening in early July 1947. The two men were sitting out after dark talking after having spent the evening

completing assorted household chores. Woody reported that they suddenly noticed that the wall of the house was lit up as if it were struck by a car's headlights. Looking round for the source of the light, they saw a brilliantly lit object hurtling through the sky. The object was heading north on a downward trajectory and seemed to hit the ground some miles away.

Woody said that the next morning he and his father got up and drove out to see if they could find the crashed object. We shall return to what they discovered later, but for now it is important why William Woody was able to make the trip. He was not at work because it was the weekend. That would make the date of his sighting of the object as the evening of Friday 4 or Saturday 5 July.

It is usually assumed that this was the same object that was seen by Ragsdale, and is treated by many researchers as confirmation that the crash happened on 4 July. However,

Woody never definitely said that he saw an object blazing through the sky on 4 July. It might have been 5 July. Just possibly he may have been referring to the following weekend, that of 11 or 12 July, in which case whatever he saw was not the crashing object that left debris on the Foster Ranch. Perhaps it was a meteor.

Much more definite regarding a date and time, but not so firm about what was seen, was the testimony supplied by two nuns working at St Mary's Hospital in Roswell. On the evening of Friday 4 July, Mother Superior Mary Bernadette and Sister Capistrano were indulging their hobby of astronomy by scanning the night sky. Their log book was discovered in the 1980s. For the time slot 11 to 11.30 pm they recorded seeing a brilliantly lit object plunge to earth to the north of their location in Roswell. They thought it might be a crippled aircraft and logged it as such, but included no detailed description of its colour, size or trajectory.

Taking all the evidence to have emerged to date, there are three suggested dates on which the object may have crashed: 14 June, 2 July and 4 July. There is evidence for and against each date. Most researchers discount the 14 June date and concentrate on one or other of the later dates. In truth, nobody can be certain when the object came down.

Rather more certain is the date on which Mac Brazel went to study the debris on his ranch in more detail. That was almost certainly on 5 July. What he found puzzled and excited him. It was quite unlike anything else that he had ever seen. On this point, nearly everyone is agreed. Sceptics point out that Brazel was an old-time rancher living on a ranch so remote that it had no electricity and no running water. On the other hand, New Mexico is not the middle of nowhere and crucially, bearing in mind the USAAF cover story that emerged a few days later, Brazel had seen weather balloons that had come down on desert land before.

At this point one of the main discrepancies in the accounts given in the 1970s and 1980s about the crucial two days after Brazel inspected the debris must be dealt with. According to Bill Brazel, two of his younger siblings were at the Foster Ranch with their father at the time. He said that Mac later dropped them off at their mother's house in Tularosa on his way to Roswell. The article in the *Roswell Daily Record* on 9 July states that when he found the debris Brazel was on his ranch with his wife and two younger children.

Speaking in the 1990s, Brazel's daughter Bessie, who was 14 in 1947, also said that she and her brother were at the Foster Ranch when the debris was found. She also claims to have accompanied her father into Roswell and not to have been dropped off at her mother's.

The Proctors are clear that the two children did not come to visit. In her later interviews, Loretta Proctor claimed that her son William had spent the day with Mac Brazel, riding the pastures to round up sheep after the previous night's storms. Loretta claimed that William had been with Mac when he inspected the debris and that Brazel paid his visit when driving young William home. According to this version the younger Brazel children were not present.

These apparently contradictory versions have caused some confusion among researchers. They have been used to discredit the accounts given by Bill Brazel, Bessie Brazel or Loretta Proctor, depending on which version the researcher prefers.

However, it must be remembered that all these versions were given some thirty or forty years after the event. All agree that the key features in their memories were the wreckage and Mac Brazel's reaction to it. It is quite

> **What he found puzzled and excited him. It was quite unlike anything else that he had ever seen.**

likely that less important features got forgotten. It may well be that the younger Brazel children were paying a visit of a few days to their father's ranch and that William Proctor went out riding sheep with Mac. If the younger children stayed at the ranch to play while William and Mac rode out working, then maybe William did not see them and did not mention them to his parents. There is no great need to believe that there is any real contradiction between the accounts.

As we shall see, Bessie's claim to have accompanied her father to Roswell does cause some problems with the generally accepted version of events that took place later. For now it is only worth mentioning that there is a dispute about her movements – although she has always been perfectly clear and consistent on the subject herself.

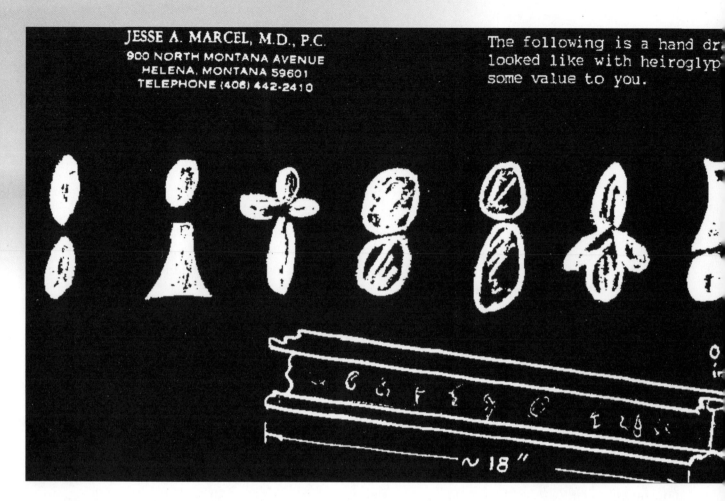

JESSE A. MARCEL, M.D., P.C.
900 NORTH MONTANA AVENUE
HELENA, MONTANA 59601
TELEPHONE (406) 442-2410

The following is a hand dr
looked like with heiroglyp
some value to you.

~ 18 "

▲ Jesse Marcel's drawing of what the light-weight struts marked with strange figures looked like. There have been different interpretations of what these might have been.

UNUSUAL DEBRIS

Brazel's actions after finding the odd debris are fairly well documented, though there are some controversies. Firstly he collected up some pieces of the wreckage and took them back to his ranch house. That evening (5 July) he went to see his neighbours, the Proctors, who lived some 10 miles (16 km) away. When interviewed in the 1970s, the Proctors recalled the visit well because Brazel – normally a fairly reserved individual – behaved in an excited fashion.

At first Mac Brazel told Floyd Proctor that he had found some odd wreckage on his ranch, didn't know what to make of it and wanted Proctor to come over to take a look. Proctor, however, had had a long hard day of his own and did not want to face the 20-mile (32 km) journey over to Brazel's house and back, so he refused to go. Brazel then began talking about the debris, describing it and emphasizing again and again how odd it was.

Brazel's description of the debris to the Proctors was the first that he was to give. The wreckage was not described in detail in any

contemporary account, so researchers have only the memories of those involved to go on. The Proctors, when interviewed in the 1970s, said that Brazel had not brought the debris with him, but said that they clearly remembered how he described it. According to this account, the debris took the form of very thin metal sheets with other fragments of what looked like paper and some short pieces of strut or stick. Brazel told them that the paper-like materials were so tough that he could not cut them with a knife, while the sheets of metal were unlike any other sort of metal he had ever seen.

At places over the debris were some sort of strange markings in a purplish or pinkish colour. Brazel likened the markings to the sort of Chinese or Japanese writing that was then printed on to firework wrappers, but that it was different. When talking some months later to his son Bill, Mac likened the markings to Native American petroglyphs that decorated some of the local rocks.

✗ Speaking in the 1990s, Loretta Proctor said that Brazel had, in fact, brought a small sample of the debris with him on his visit. She

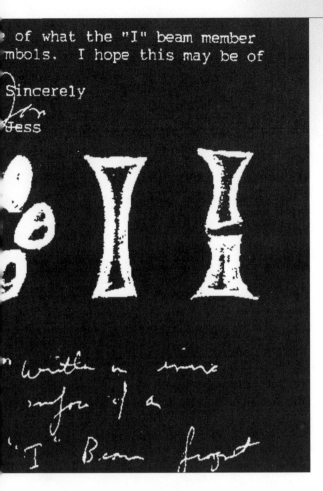

of what the "I" beam member
mbols. I hope this may be of

Sincerely

Jess

"written on inside
surface of a
'I' Beam fragment

said that the sample consisted of a small sheet of the metal. The metal was very thin, almost like foil, but had a most curious property. 'When you crushed it, it straightened back out. It wouldn't stay crushed.' She said that Brazel had tried to whittle the struts with his knife, but had made no impression. Nor had he been able to set fire to them with a match.

Brazel stayed at the Proctor ranch for some time discussing his finds. In the end, according to the Proctors, it was decided that Brazel should take the debris into Roswell. Brazel said he would do so next time he was in town. The impression gained is that Brazel was deeply puzzled by his find, but was not treating the matter with any great urgency.

Bessie claims that she also saw and handled the debris while it was on the Foster Ranch. Interviewed in 1979, she recalled debris not very different from that described by the Proctors. She too said that it came in three forms: thin metal foil sheeting, another sheeting with the appearance of thick paper, and some pieces of strutting. She said that none of it could be cut, and that it did not resemble anything she had ever seen before. In particu-

lar, Bessie discounted the idea that it had come from a weather balloon. 'We had seen weather balloons quite a lot, both on the ground and in the air. This was nothing like that.'

She also described the markings in detail. These were, she said, impossible to decipher but she rather got the impression that they were numbers. This was because they were laid out in vertical columns the way she wrote out numbers when doing addition sums at school. There were also different sets of markings that looked like pictures of flowers, but heavily stylized.

Bill Brazel, the adult son of Mac, did not appear on the scene until a few days later. He did not see the debris collected by his father but did pick up some other pieces that he found out on the pasture himself. These were, he recalled in 1979, fairly consistent with what his father had reported. The thin metal sheeting, he said, had the dull, dark colour of lead sheet, but was as thin as aluminium foil and was so lightweight that it was almost as if it wasn't there. Furthermore, he agreed with Mrs Proctor about its most unusual property, saying 'you could wrinkle it and lay it back down and it immediately resumed its original shape'.

Bill also mentioned the struts. He said that they looked a bit like balsa wood, but were of a much darker colour and were immensely strong. He was unable to scratch or mark them in any way, or to break or snap them. As for weight, they were as lightweight as the foil.

Bill did not mention the paper-like debris, but did come across some threads. These were, he said, of a similar thickness to the cotton used to sew buttons on to shirts and again were very lightweight and very strong. He said that he had held a piece of the thread in his two hands and tried to snap it, but had been completely unable to make an impression on it.

As we shall see when dealing with the

retrieval of the crashed object, Marcel also saw and handled the debris found at the Foster Ranch. While the Brazels and Proctors were rural folk who had handled the odd weather balloon when it had come down, but who might otherwise be dismissed as not entirely up to date with all the modern inventions of the time, Major Marcel was a serving intelligence officer in the USAAF. It was part of his job to be fully conversant with all types of flying vehicle whether it was of American or foreign origin. He too has been consistently adamant that the wreckage was not something that he had ever encountered.

Speaking in 1979, Marcel gave a rather more detailed description of what he had found than did the other witnesses. He did not recall any thread-like material but did

> **"Marcel said that the metal sheeting was possible to bend, even to wrinkle up, but that it would not stay bent.**

describe the paper-like fabric, the metal foil and the struts – including the markings.

According to Marcel, the struts were about half an inch (13 mm) thick, shaped rather like an 'I' and were extremely tough. He recalled that it was possible to flex them, but not to break them or to set them on fire. The paper-like material – he likened it to parchment – was brown and incredibly strong. Some of the purple markings were on this material, and Marcel described them as being like hieroglyphs that had been painted on. Like the struts, the parchment-type fabric would not burn when a match was held to it.

The metal sheeting, however, impressed him the most. It was, he said, as thin as the metal foil in a cigarette packet, but even lighter. He said that a piece about 2 ft by 1 ft (60 cm by 30 cm) was so light that he could

pick it up and barely notice it was there. And yet it was astonishingly strong. He said that it was possible to bend it, even to wrinkle it up, but that it would not stay bent. He and his colleagues were so intrigued that they tried to cut it, but failed. Then they took a 16lb (7 kg) sledgehammer to it, but failed to dent it at all.

Having collected some of the debris and visited the Proctor ranch, Mac Brazel returned to his home on the evening of 5 July – where his two younger children were presumably staying. According to Bill Brazel, Mac spent the next day on his ranch, but that evening he drove into Corona to see his brother-in-law Hollis Wilson. Corona was, and is, a small township lacking the facilities to be found in Roswell. None of the witnesses say where the children were, but it would make sense if Mac took them to see their uncle.

After having discussed the situation with Hollis and a friend of his from Alamogordo – Bill Brazel could not recall his name – Mac Brazel decided to take some of the debris into Roswell and report it.

The impression gained at this point is that Mac was now treating the matter rather more seriously than he had done the previous evening at the Proctor Ranch. Bill Brazel said that he thought the reason for this was something that the man from Alamogordo had told him. As we have already seen, the first rash of reports of flying saucers was sweeping across America at this time, and a disproportionate number of the early sightings were being reported from the south-western states. There was a huge amount of speculation going on about what these objects were, where they came from and what they were doing.

However, the very first report had been made by Kenneth Arnold on 24 June 1947, only 11 days before Mac Brazel's trip into Corona. Bill Brazel was of the opinion that his father had not heard anything about flying saucers at all, and that the man from Alamogordo was the first person to tell him

about these apparently hugely futuristic aircraft flying about. The three men seem to have put two and two together. Highly advanced flying craft were being seen in the area, and here was Mac Brazel having found apparently highly advanced wreckage that had fallen from the sky. Perhaps the two were linked. Perhaps the wreckage had come from a flying saucer. It was, the men decided,

important that Brazel report the matter sooner rather than later. Rather than leave it until the next time he was in Roswell, Brazel decided to go as soon as possible.

REPORTING THE FIND

That evening he went back to his ranch ready to face the long drive into Roswell the next

▲ Kenneth Arnold points to an illustration showing the shape and configuration of the mysterious aircraft that he saw in 1947.

day. According to Bill Brazel, his father first dropped off the children at Tularosa before heading to Roswell. Although the contemporary reports in the *Roswell Daily Record* stated that Mac Brazel was going into town to sell wool, Bill disagreed. He maintained that his father sold his wool under contract and that the buyers always came to collect it from his ranch. Bill said that he thought his father had

"One morning Barnett emerged from his tent to see sunlight glinting off a large metallic object over a mile away.

gone into Roswell to inquire about buying a new pick-up truck as his existing vehicle was getting rather old and unreliable. However, the newspaper report should not be discounted entirely. Perhaps Mac put through a phone call to the wool merchants while he was in town, as his ranch lacked a phone as well as electricity.

Once in Roswell, Mac Brazel went to see Sheriff George Wilcox to report his find. He took with him a few pieces of the debris to show how peculiar it all was. Thereafter the story of Mac Brazel's debris becomes part of the story of the retrieval of the crashed object, which will be dealt with in the next chapter.

Meanwhile, there was apparently a second crash site. Whatever Brazel's debris was, everyone agrees that it took the form of a large number of fairly small fragments scattered over a large area of pasture on the Foster Ranch. It was this that seems to have been the main focus of all the contemporary press reports, but even then there had been hints of something else being found. As researchers began to investigate the Roswell Incident these hints began to take more definite form.

It will be recalled that the first report concerning a UFO crash in New Mexico (which was found by Stanton Friedman after he

spoke to Jesse Marcel) came from Lydia Sleppy, who was reporting a telephone conversation she had had with radio reporter Johnny McBoyle. McBoyle had apparently said that he had seen a crashed saucer that looked like 'a big, crumpled dishpan' and that other people had told him 'something about little men on board'.

McBoyle had died by the time the investigation began, and other than Sleppy nobody could recall his talking about a crashed UFO. But it soon transpired that McBoyle was not the only witness to have seen a crashed saucer. There was also Grady L. Barnett, widely known as Barney. In 1947, Barnett had been a civil engineer working for the US Soil Conservation Service. In an arid area such as New Mexico the health of the underlying soil was of prime concern to farmers and ranchers as well as to the state and federal authorities. It was, after all, only twenty or so years since the 'dustbowl' disaster had seen hundreds of square miles of productive farmland reduced to worthless desert by a combination of poor farming practices and years of successive low rainfall. Barnett was a well-trained scientist doing an important job in a challenging environment.

Unfortunately, Barney Barnett had also died in the intervening time (in 1969) but he had spoken to his friends about his experiences and they could recall some details clearly enough. As the early researchers put the Barnett story together, it ran as follows:

Some time in 1947 or 1948, Barnett had been working out of Socorro conducting soil tests in an area of rolling prairie that he called 'the flats'. One morning he emerged from his tent to see sunlight glinting off a large metallic object over a mile away that he was certain had not been there the night before. Thinking that an aircraft may have crashed overnight, Barnett got dressed and trudged off to investigate. When he reached the object he realized that it was something rather odd. It was resting against a slope and was clearly badly damaged. There was what looked like a large rent torn in the side as if ripped open by the impact or perhaps an explosion.

The object was made of a dull, silvery metal that reminded Barnett of dirty stainless steel. It was not very big, perhaps some 30 ft (9 m) across. There were no wings, tailfin or wheels to be seen, only the damaged fuselage. The object was rounded in shape; some people thought Barnett had said it was completely round like a disk.

As Barnett was looking at the strange object and wondering what to do, he saw a group of men approaching on foot from another direction. He went to meet them and learned that they were a team of archaeologists who were working on a nearby Native American site. They too had seen the strange object in the dawn light and had come over to investigate. One person claimed that Barnett had said

that they came from the University of Pennsylvania, or some other 'fancy Eastern university'. While Barnett was chatting to some of the archaeologists, others had gone to investigate the crashed object at close quarters. They called out that there were dead bodies in and next to the craft.

STRANGE CORPSES

Barnett then walked towards the object to get a closer look. He said that the dead bodies were of creatures that were similar to – but were too small to be – adult humans. Their heads were large in proportion to their bodies and totally hairless. Their eyes were small and oddly positioned. They wore one-piece suits without any obvious fastenings in the form of buttons or zips.

Barnett admitted that he did not get a very

◀ Most eye-witness accounts of meetings with aliens describe them as wearing tight, one-piece costumes – just as reported by the witnesses to bodies found at Roswell.

▲ The Sacramento Mountains of New Mexico would have presented a difficult obstacle for a crippled aircraft at low altitude.

close look at the bodies because at that point a military officer came hurrying up in a jeep. The officer leapt down and 'took control'. He ushered Barnett and the archaeologists away from the crash, telling them that the incident was a military matter and that they would have to leave the area. As Barnett set off to walk back to his camp he said that other jeeps and trucks began to arrive. Military personnel scrambled out to cordon off the area.

There were, of course, immediate problems with the Barnett story. The first was the lack of a firm date when it took place. The closest that anyone could place it was somewhere in 1947 or 1948; some were not certain even of that and said that it could have been any time

to assume that the site had been somewhere near that town. He had described the place as 'the flats', a term in use in the region to describe an area of prairie or fairly level ground, in contrast to hills or mountains. This was all frustratingly vague, but then one researcher spotted a place named The Flats located on the Plains of San Agustin to the west of Socorro. If Barnett had meant The Flats instead of the more generic 'the flats', then the researchers had found the location of the crash he had witnessed.

Despite the fact that the Barnett story was at first sight highly unlikely, several factors counted in favour of it being largely true – although researchers were aware of the fact that second-hand testimony of this type is always prone to confusion. The first was that

Bill Brazel reported that his father had heard a loud explosion the night before he had first noticed debris on the pasture land.

Barnett had repeated the tale only to close friends and in a serious and restrained way. This was not a tale that was boasted of late at night in bars. Secondly, everyone who had known Barnett spoke of him very highly. His former colleagues and managers said he was utterly reliable and trustworthy, as did a former sheriff of Socorro County who knew him well.

At this point in the investigation, researchers were placing the crash as having happened on 2 July because of the Wilmot sighting. That sighting had been of a UFO heading north-west from Roswell towards the Foster Ranch. Bill Brazel reported that his father had heard a loud explosion the night before he had first noticed debris on the pasture land.

between the end of the war and 1951. While it was tempting to link this apparent saucer crash to the Brazel-Roswell story there was no proof that the two had happened at the same time.

Another key problem was the location of the crashed object that Barnett had seen. Barnett had said that he was based in Socorro at the time, so it might have been reasonable

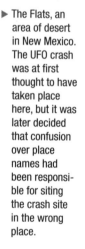

Despite the ambiguities over the dates, the researchers now put together a tentative scenario. The UFO had been flying north-west over south-eastern New Mexico. It passed over Roswell at a little before 10 pm. When it reached the Foster Ranch a few minutes later it had suffered a severe malfunction of some kind that caused an explosion on board. That explosion was heard by Mac Brazel and blew out a mass of debris and wreckage that fell over the pasture where Brazel spotted it the next morning. The crippled UFO had flown on, now heading more west than north-west. It managed to get over the Sacramento Mountains, but then lost height and crashed into the ground at The Flats on the Plains of San Agustin.

If Barnett had passed away, his tale left open the tantalizing possibility that at least some of the archaeologists that he had met on the crash site were still alive and would be able to tell their tales. This set the researchers off on a search for the archaeologists that would consume much time and energy for little result. The first and most obvious port of call was the University of Pennsylvania archaeology department. It was soon discovered that they had not had any teams working near Socorro in July 1947.

The next targets for research were the University of New Mexico and the Museum of New Mexico. In theory these institutions were supposed to be kept informed by other academic bodies doing scientific field work in the state. Archaeological work on a Native American site would certainly fall under this heading. However, the researchers were warned that not all academic bodies were as careful over notification as they should have been, and in any case there was no guarantee that records from the 1940s were complete. Nevertheless, several archaeological teams were identified as being active in the Socorro area in the summer of 1947. Team members were contacted and interviewed, but all denied any knowledge of any unusual aircraft crash.

▶ The Flats, an area of desert in New Mexico. The UFO crash was at first thought to have taken place here, but it was later decided that confusion over place names had been responsible for siting the crash site in the wrong place.

The Crash

In 1990, researcher Kevin Randle was contacted by a man who would not give his name, but said that he had heard through the academic grapevine that Randle was looking for archaeologists who had seen a strange air crash in New Mexico in 1947. While all anonymous information must be treated with suspicion, and is generally excluded from this book, this particular call proved to be very interesting.

The man said that he had been part of an archaeological team in July 1947, but that he had not been working on the Plains of San Agustin or even near Socorro. He had been in Lincoln County, north of Roswell. He said that he and his colleagues had one morning been 'field walking', that is, walking across open country looking for archaeological clues on the surface, when they had come across a man standing alone on a rise. The man had been looking down a slope towards what appeared to be a crashed and crumpled aircraft fuselage, but that the aircraft had appeared to be very odd as it had no wings. The anonymous caller then said that one of his colleagues had spotted some dead bodies. These were described as being short with large heads and wearing a silvery uniform of some kind. The caller said he had not got a good look himself as at that point a couple of jeeps had pulled up and an army officer had ordered them to clear the site.

The man said the army officer had marched him and his colleagues off a short distance and then taken down their names and addresses. The officer had then threatened that the government would cut all research funds to anyone who talked about what they had seen. The witness hung up without leaving either a name or contact details.

The call seemed to generally support the Barnett story, though seen from the point of view of the archaeologists. Any discrepancies, such as the man saying two jeeps pulled up while Barnett had claimed only one, could be easily put down to varying memories of events. The main weakness in the story was that the outline of the Barnett story, though not its detail, had already been published in the 1980 book by Berlitz and Moore. The caller may simply have been a prankster who had read that account, invented a few extra details and made the call for mischievous reasons.

> ## The officer had then threatened that the government would cut all research funds to anyone who talked about what they had seen.

However, there had long been the nagging worry among researchers that the Barnett story had been located at the wrong place and the evidence pointing to the Plains of San Agustin was merely circumstantial. The anonymous caller's location of the site in Lincoln County added to this feeling. When other witnesses to the crash started coming forward, the idea that the UFO had actually crashed on the Plains of San Agustin fell out of favour.

A key witness in this development was Jim Ragsdale. As outlined above, Ragsdale said that he and his companion were camping about 40 miles (65 km) north of Roswell on the night of 4 July when he saw a blazing object plunge to Earth. Ragsdale had then claimed that he and his friend had left their tent and gone to investigate. Both of them had been drinking, Ragsdale said, so he drove his car carefully along a dirt road. As they came over a crest, they saw, some distance off, a metallic craft crumpled up against the foot of a rise.

Ragsdale claimed that he had set off on foot with a flashlight, but the batteries had given out, leaving him with only starlight to guide him. He was unwilling to walk far

▶ Jim Ragsdale claimed that he was camping outside Roswell when he saw a mysterious object crash from the sky.

across broken scrubland in such conditions. He peered at the craft and listened carefully. He saw no signs of movement and heard no cries for help. Concluding that any occupants had either walked off or been killed in the impact, Ragsdale returned to his car and drove back to the tent where he and his companion spent the rest of the night.

This account by Ragsdale placed a crash by a metallic, silvery-coloured aircraft of a strange, wingless design just north of Roswell on or close to the date when Brazel first saw the debris on his land. Taken with the Woody sighting and the records kept by the nuns, this indicated that the crash had taken place north of Roswell and not on the Plains of San Agustin at all. The anonymous caller, for what his evidence was worth, concurred.

ARCHAEOLOGIST WITNESS

The hunt for the missing archaeologists was back on – this time looking for a team working north of Roswell on 4 July 1947. Eventually it was found that a team had been active in the area at about the right time, led by Dr William Curry Holden of the Texas Tech University. The records were vague as to when the team had left for the New Mexico desert, but did show that they had returned by 9 July.

Kevin Randle interviewed Dr Holden in 1992. The interview has proved to be controversial because by this date Holden was 96 years old and would die a few months later. Sceptics have alleged that he may have been confused about events, easily led or otherwise unreliable. However the sceptics were not there and Randle was. He reported that Holden 'seemed to be in good health, living at home and moved easily ... seemed to have a firm grasp on the situation'.

During the interview, Holden stated: 'I was there. I saw it all, but it was so long ago.' He admitted that he could not recall much detail about events, but confirmed that he and some students had been working north of Roswell somewhere when one morning they found an unusual object that looked as if it was an aircraft that had crashed. He said he had not got closer than about 60 yd (55 m) from the object, which he described as being rounded in the front and scalloped at the rear while lacking wings in the conventional sense. He thought that there may have been some bodies, but was not sure.

Holden recalled that one of his students had gone off to find a phone and call the authorities and that a short while later some soldiers had arrived. An officer told Holden that the object was important to national security and asked him to keep quiet about the find. Holden had assumed that the craft was some experimental aircraft and had accordingly not spread the story.

In fact he had mentioned it in passing to a colleague named Dr Charles Schultz who had been driving through New Mexico some days later. Schultz had passed through Roswell and, north of the town, had seen soldiers apparently blocking off access to the desert roads. He mentioned this a few weeks later to Holden, knowing that he had also been in the area, and Holden replied that it may have had something to do with a strange aircraft crash he had seen.

> **An officer told Holden that the object was important to national security and asked him to keep quiet about the find.**

NEW WITNESS

In 1990 a spectacular new piece of evidence emerged when Gerald Anderson, often called Gerry Anderson, phoned Randle as a result of the 1989 television show. Anderson later gave interviews to both press and broadcast media in which he made increasingly dramatic claims. Some of the background detail given by Anderson has since proved to be false. The fact that he claimed to remember with total clarity events that took place 43 years earlier when he was aged only 5 added further suspicion. While there is no evidence that proves that Anderson's story is a total invention, most researchers prefer to treat it as unsub-

stantiated and ignore it. A few, however, do lend credence to Anderson's claims, so the story is worth covering.

Anderson places his experiences on the Plains of San Agustin on the morning of 5 July. According to Anderson he and his uncle, who was named Ted, had been on a camping holiday in the Roswell area in early July. At dawn on 5 July they found a large, silvery object resting against a small hill with four bodies scattered around it. Two of the bodies were clearly dead, and a third was badly injured, but the fourth appeared unhurt and was apparently seeking to help its wounded

Moments later a couple of army vehicles pulled up and everyone was shepherded away from the scene so that they could see no more.

companion. Anderson says that he moved closer to the craft and found that it was emanating a severe chill, rather as if he were standing in front of an open freezer.

Uncle Ted was approaching the two living entities. They clearly failed to understand Uncle Ted's offers of help and the young Anderson assumed that they were foreigners who did not speak English. At this point a group of around half a dozen men appeared over the hill. Anderson thought that their leader, a tall balding man, said his name was 'Buskirk' or something similar. The new arrivals joined Uncle Ted in trying to help the wounded humanoid, but were waved away by its uninjured companion. Then a single, older man arrived on foot. Moments later a couple of army vehicles pulled up and everyone was shepherded away from the scene so that they could see no more.

Anderson went on to describe the humanoids that he claimed he saw at the crash site.

He said that they were rather taller than he had been at the time – which would have put them a little over 4 ft (1.2 m) tall. They had heads that were bald and much too large for their bodies, while their arms and legs were thin and spindly. He said that their eyes were very large, oval-shaped and jet black. In other words he was describing the 'Grey' type of alien that by the 1990s was dominating UFO literature as it increasingly concentrated on abduction cases.

Researchers soon found problems relating to Anderson's account. If he were talking about the same event related by Barnett, then the men led by 'Buskirk' were the missing archaeologists. It did not take long to find an archaeologist of the correct name: Dr Win Buskirk of Arizona. He was even rather tall and had started going bald as a young man in the 1940s. However, Buskirk was able to prove that he had been in Arizona in the summer of 1947, and in any case denied having ever found a crashed aircraft or UFO of any kind. It transpired that in 1957 Buskirk had taught a term at a local high school – and one of the students had been a teenaged Anderson.

Anderson produced a diary that had, he said, belonged to his Uncle Ted. This did not mention the UFO crash, but did detail the camping trip near Roswell in July 1947. Scientific tests proved that the relevant pages had been written in an ink not invented until the later 1950s. When that news broke, most researchers discarded Anderson's account as worthless – though some still hold that it is valuable.

CHANGING STORY

Meanwhile, Ragsdale had changed his story by 1995. In his original version, which several of his friends remembered him telling them long before the researchers began work, he and his female companion had left the area early the following morning. Apparently they were worried by the strange events of the night before and did not want to be found alone out in the desert together. Again there was a vague hint that Ragsdale was a bit wary of revealing too much about the girl and his relationship with her.

In his new version, however, Ragsdale and his companion returned to the object that they had seen in the distance the night before. Although the girl was wary of the object, fearing it was a bomb that might explode, Ragsdale walked over the desert to inspect it. He found a dull, silvery craft about 60 ft (18 m) long. He said it was shaped like a 'V', with very narrow wings along the sides. The point of the V was embedded in the side of the slope and was badly crumpled up. A few pieces of debris lay about. Ragsdale says he picked up a small sheet of metal and was amazed at how light it was. He bent it, but it sprang back to its original shape.

Ragsdale also says that he saw 'bodies or something, they looked like bodies' lying beside the craft. These were, he said, about 4 ft (1.2 m) tall with abnormally large heads. Their eyes were, he said, oval and intensely black. Like Anderson, this new version of events by Ragsdale is describing the 'Greys', which featured strongly in UFO writing in the 1990s.

At this point, Ragsdale says, he heard motor engines and turned to see a jeep approaching followed by two trucks. Ragsdale sprinted back to where his companion was waiting in their vehicle. Together they watched while a squad of military men leapt down from the trucks. An officer had a quick look at the crashed object and then ordered the men to fan out. They seemed to be searching the area and were armed. Ragsdale and his companion drove off and did not return.

As can be clearly seen there are discrepancies between these various versions of what happened at the site of an alleged crashed flying craft. Barnett mentions a team of archaeologists, but nobody else before the

army arrives. Holden mentions a man, presumably Barnett, but nobody else. These two accounts match, but neither Barnett nor Holden specified a date. Ragsdale does give a firm date, but makes it clear that he was alone at the crash site when the army arrived – there is no sign of Barnett or the archaeologists. Anderson mentions both the archaeologists

and Barnett, but not Ragsdale, though he is not mentioned by either of them. The anonymous caller talked about a man who may have been Barnett, but not Anderson or Ragsdale.

The different accounts cannot all be correct, and sceptics would argue that none of them are credible or reliable. However, on one point all the accounts are in agreement.

Within two or three hours of dawn, the military were on the scene and were clearing the area of civilians. This accords well with both contemporary press accounts and numerous other witness statements made later.

Whatever it was that crashed near Roswell was impounded by the military. Quite clearly a highly secretive retrieval was under way.

▲ The crash site scene as described by Jim Ragsdale in his revised account of the events outside Roswell.

4

The Crash Site Retrieval

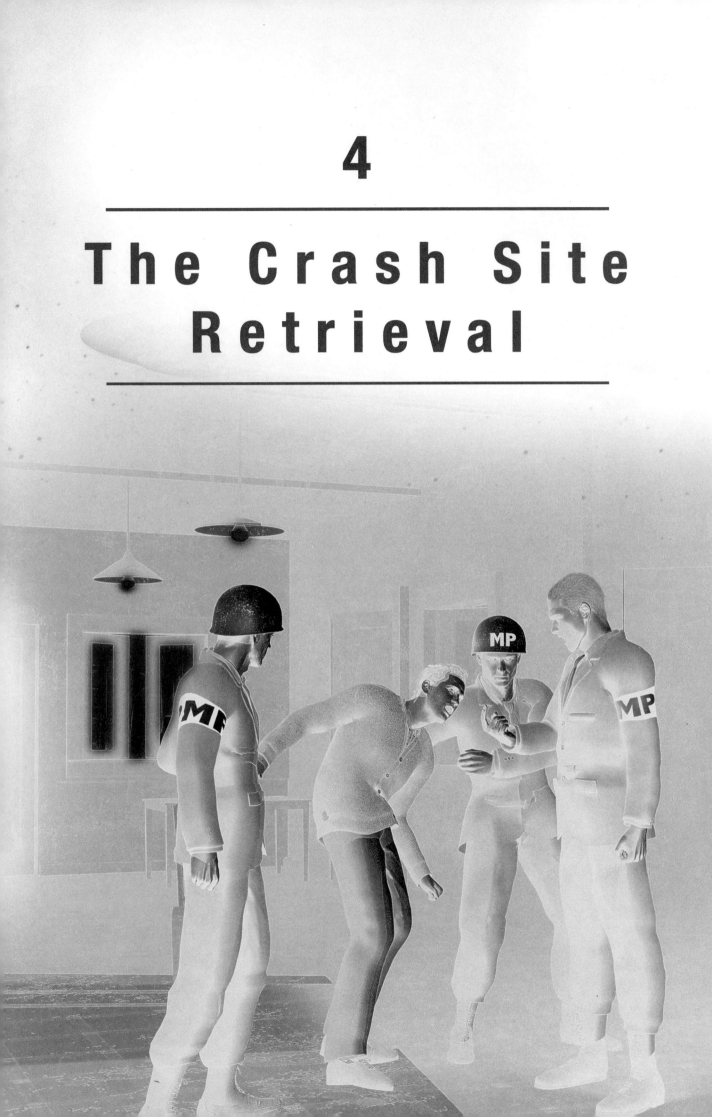

NOBODY DISPUTES that whatever crashed at Roswell in July 1947 was collected by the USAAF and taken away for study. The USAAF have said as much themselves. The disputes centre around what was retrieved, where it was taken and what happened to it afterwards.

As we have seen there appear to have been two distinct crash sites. First there was what has become known as the 'Debris Field' on the Foster Ranch. This was the area discovered by Mac Brazel and investigated by him on either 3 or 5 July, depending on which date is accepted for the crash. The material found here seems to have been small pieces of debris scattered over a fairly large area.

The second site has become known as the 'Crash Site'. This was where Barnett, Ragsdale and others reported seeing a crumpled, metallic craft of some kind. Any wreckage recovered from here would be much more substantial than that found on the Debris Field and, if the eyewitness accounts can be trusted, would include three or more bodies.

Time-Lag

Looking at the contemporary accounts found in newspapers at the time, it is clear that most – if not all – public statements made by the USAAF at the time referred to the Debris Field. This is odd and has been at the centre of many of the disputes and allegations concerning the retrieval.

According to the chronology of events as put together by UFO researchers in the 1980s and since, rancher Mac Brazel did not report his finds until at least four days after the crash, possibly rather longer. And yet all the witnesses who claim to have seen the Crash Site insist that the military were on the site on the morning after the crash. So the USAAF would have known about the crash and would have begun their retrieval of the

◀ The sign erected recently outside Roswell to guide visitors to what is now generally thought to have been the Crash Site, as described by witnesses.

▲ The anonymous student archaeologist hurried to a gas station, using the public pay phone there to alert the authorities to the crashed UFO.

wreckage several days before Brazel arrived in Roswell to report his find.

It is this time lag that goes to the heart of the alleged cover-up conspiracy surrounding the declared Roswell UFO crash. Those researchers who believe that the USAAF covered up the facts surrounding the UFO crash and have been keeping it secret ever since have put together the following timeline for events:

The UFO, if such it was, crashed on the night of 2 or 4 July.

The USAAF were alerted to the crash almost immediately and search parties were sent out at dawn the next day, finding the downed craft an hour or so after first light.

They found civilians on the site, but ushered them away and advised them not to say anything about the events.

It was only when Brazel turned up in Roswell to report his finds that the USAAF

realized that they would be unable keep the crash a secret.

The USAAF concocted a cover story to hide the truth and put the press and public off the trail – which they successfully did for the next thirty years.

As theories go, it is at least interesting and does explain how the military could be throwing a cordon around the crash site some days before they were apparently alerted to the existence of the crash by Brazel. The key question must be, is there any evidence for this suggested chain of events?

There is, in fact, plenty of evidence, but not all of it is accepted by all researchers. As so often with events around Roswell it depends on who the researcher is willing to believe.

It is probably best to start with the evidence presented by Major Jesse Marcel. He was the intelligence officer at the Roswell air base at the time. If anything unusual occurred, he would be the first person to be alerted to it. This is, in fact, what happened when Sheriff

Wilcox phoned the air base to report that Brazel was in his office with some strange debris that appeared to have come from an aircraft. The call was put through to Marcel.

Yet Marcel is adamant that he had heard nothing about any strange crash before he got Wilcox's call. Sceptics have used this fact to suggest that there was no crashed UFO at the Crash Site at all, but this is not necessarily the case. Any call from a member of the public would have gone to Marcel, but not information originating from within the USAAF. In 1947, Marcel held the rank of Major. This may be a senior rank when it came to the running of an operational air base such as Roswell, but was fairly junior in the scheme of the higher command of the USAAF. If there was any important secret inside the USAAF it is unlikely that it would be discussed with a Major unless he was directly involved. If a crashed UFO had been found by USAAF personnel from a base other than Roswell then Marcel would almost certainly not have been informed about it. This is exactly what is alleged to have happened.

Before looking at the evidence for the secretive retrieval that is supposed to have taken place, there is one often overlooked loose end that should be studied. Barnett, Holden and the anonymous caller claiming to have been an archaeologist on the site all said that one of the archaeology students went off to call the authorities about an hour or so after dawn. They also state that the military officer and his backup began arriving very soon afterwards.

Now back in 1947 there were no mobile phones, still fewer satellite phones, and no archaeology team out on a dig is known to have had a two-way radio – certainly it was not standard kit. The only way the student could have alerted the authorities to the crash was to get in a car, drive to the nearest township or motor garage and make a phone call. Given the position of the alleged Crash Site,

that would have taken at least an hour and possibly longer. Then the authorities would have to respond to the call, using up at least another hour or more even if they thought they were dealing with a conventional aircraft crash with wounded survivors.

It should have taken at least two hours, maybe three or four, before the authorities alerted by the student could have reached the Crash Site. And yet everyone is agreed that the military arrived quickly, within less than half an hour or so.

Moreover, the student is not described in any witness statement as having returned to the Crash Site before the military turned up.

It should have taken at least two hours, maybe three or four, before the authorities alerted by the student could have reached the Crash Site.

This is, in fact, hardly surprising as he was in all likelihood still in a car bumping over the unmetalled desert roads on his way to a telephone when the army officer reached the scene.

That leads to two questions. Firstly, how did the military know about the crash in time to turn up so early? And secondly, what happened to the student and the authorities that he called?

It is the second question that is the easier to answer, and so will be dealt with first. Arriving at whichever phone he decided to head for, the student would most likely have called the nearest sheriff's office. Bear in mind that at the time the student left the Crash Site, he and his colleagues thought that they had discovered a crashed aircraft of some kind. The nearest sheriff was George Wilcox in Roswell. If Wilcox thought he was dealing

▶ In July 1947, the Roswell Fire Department was called out to attend what was at first thought to be a crashed aircraft in the desert. They were not allowed to approach the object by US military personnel who had reached the site first. This event is usually linked to the Crash Site.

with a crashed aircraft, standard procedure would have been to send out a deputy to investigate and to alert the local fire department and hospital.

Strictly speaking, the Roswell Fire Department was responsible only for fires and emergencies that took place within Roswell. The Crash Site was in Lincoln County and so was not really their affair. However, they were an emergency service and if an emergency took place in which lives might be at risk they were unlikely to bother too much with county boundaries, especially if they had the nearest fire engine on duty. Certainly on other dates, the Roswell Fire Department sent out men and equipment to deal with fires outside their official territory. To argue, as some sceptics have done, that the Roswell Fire Department would not have attended an air crash in Lincoln County is not sustainable.

Firefighter's Daughter

The key witness in tracking the results of the student's phone call is Frankie Rowe, daughter of Dan Dwyer, who, in the summer of 1947, was a firefighter with the Roswell Fire Department. In 1947, Frankie was a school-

girl attending school in Roswell. She was in the habit of going to the fire station after school so that her father could give her a lift home when he came off duty.

One day in July 1947 (she could not recall the precise date when interviewed in 1993), Frankie went to meet her father after school only to find that he was out on an emergency call. She sat down to wait. While she waited a state trooper arrived. The policeman, whose name she did not remember, said that her father would not be long. He had been called out to attend an air crash north of the town, but that the fire crew was not needed and was packing up its equipment.

The policeman then showed her a strange piece of metal that he said he had picked up at the crash site. According to Frankie, the metal was astonishingly lightweight and very thin. She remembered the policeman screwing it up into a ball in his hands and then letting it go again, and the metal springing back to its original shape.

When Frankie's father, Dan Dwyer, returned to the station, he told her about his trip. The crashed aircraft had been cordoned off by the military when the firefighters arrived and they had not been allowed to approach. Small pieces of wreckage were within view, and so were two sealed-up body bags from which Dwyer concluded that at least two people had been killed in the crash. Dwyer also said that there was a survivor, which looked to be about the size of a 10-year-old child but looked 'odd'. It seemed to be bald for a start.

A few days later some USAAF men called at the Dwyer house to talk to Dan Dwyer. When they learned that Frankie had seen a piece of the wreckage she was called in to the room. They were told very seriously that what they had seen was a matter of the gravest national security and that they must not talk about it to anybody. Frankie later recalled that the military men had threatened them saying that they might 'be taken out into the desert never to return'. Thereafter Dan Dwyer refused to discuss what had happened with his family or with anyone else.

Although Frankie Rowe could not recall the date on which her father had been called out to an aircraft crash north of Roswell, other than that she thought it was in July 1947, most researchers have chosen to link the event to the UFO crash. It is assumed that the fire engine was sent out in response to the call from the student. If this was the case then the emergency vehicle would have arrived on the scene about two or three hours after the student left the site, and more than an hour after the military arrived. The fire crew would, as Dan Dwyer reported, have found the site cordoned off and been unable to approach.

Some researchers also place the call made by Johnny McBoyle to Lydia Sleppy on this day. Assuming that he was talking about the same crash, this timing would fit with his description of a crashed and unidentified aircraft 'shaped like a dishpan'. Other researchers, however, believe that his reference to a rancher being involved places the call after Brazel had reported his find to Sheriff Wilcox. Sleppy cannot recall the date of the call, so its precise timing is unclear.

Wreckage Under Guard

Another witness whose testimony seems to indicate that the military were on the Crash Site very quickly is William Woody. On the day after seeing an object fall from the sky, Woody and his father had decided to drive north of Roswell to see if they could find any wreckage. They drove along Highway 285 towards Vaughn and soon became aware that all the side roads leading off into the desert to the west were guarded by military men. The Woodys tried to drive down one, but were stopped by the armed personnel and turned back. The guards blocking the desert roads were also seen by Charles Schultz.

What was going on behind that cordon of armed military guards, none of the civilian witnesses could know. The military cordon was, apparently, under the orders of Major Edwin Easley, the Provost Marshal on Roswell air base in July 1947. When he was interviewed in the 1980s about the Roswell

◀ Major Edwin Easley would have been responsible for sealing off the Crash Site from civilians, but would not necessarily have known what was happening within the cordon he established.

Incident, Easley confirmed that he had been in charge of the military police at Roswell at the time, and that part of his duties had involved mounting guards off the base when necessary. This had involved fairly routine events such as visits by senior officers and politicians, but also included air crashes and other out-of-the-way events that might be of interest to the military.

Easley did recall being requested to mount a guard over a crashed aircraft of some kind north of Roswell in the summer of 1947. His memories were vague due to the passing years and to the fact that he had not given the event much importance at the time. He said that he had deployed his men to seal off from the public a fairly large area of desert north of Roswell. He thought that he may have caught a glimpse of the crashed craft, and that it did not look like any conventional aircraft with which he was familiar. Easley's main task, however, was to post and maintain the security cordon and not to bother with what was going on inside it.

BEHIND THE LINES

In 1990 a witness still living in Roswell came forward who claimed to have been on the inside of the cordon. This man at first insisted that his name should not be revealed in public. He was quite happy to talk to researchers on the record, but was reluctant to have his name bandied about among his neighbours. In one magazine article the man was named as Joseph Osborn. In the 1991 book by Randle and Schmitt he is named as Steve MacKenzie. Other researchers referred to him as an anonymous radar operator.

The man was, in fact, Frank Kaufmann, a highly respected businessman in New Mexico who for some years was the head of the Roswell Chamber of Commerce. By the time he came forward to tell his story he was in his early seventies and retired, but still living in Roswell and active in the community. Researchers could understand why he wanted his name kept secret.

Kaufmann had been living in Roswell in 1947 and, according to his own account, was working on a part-time and informal basis for the USAAF at Roswell. During the recently ended war, Kaufmann had served in the USAAF in a variety of capacities, ending the war in 1945 as a sergeant. He had then left the military, but retained some links. A photo of him being presented with an award appeared in the *1947 Roswell USAAF Yearbook*. It is known that the USAAF did use civilian staff from time to time, either for menial duties or if they were temporarily short of staff due to sickness or some other reason. Such civilians were employed only on low-security tasks. Right from the start, Kaufmann claimed to have been employed primarily on radar duties. This fact caused some to doubt his story for radar duty at a high-profile military base such as Roswell was not a low-security task.

Since Kaufmann's death in 2001 it has been proved that he had been lying about some aspects of his story. A letter that he produced, signed by Major Edwin Easley and dated 1947, turned out to be a forgery made in the 1980s. Other documents he produced relating to his supposed employment on radar duties between 1945 and 1948 also turned out to be forged.

It is now generally agreed by most researchers that Kaufmann was not telling the truth. Why he should have concocted such an elaborate story, backed up by forged documents put together with painstaking care on period paper and using contemporary inks, can only be guessed at. It has been suggested

> **Since Kaufmann's death in 2001 it has been proved that he had been lying about some aspects of his story.**

◄ Frank Kaufmann claimed that in 1947 he saw many key aspects of the Roswell UFO crash, but since his death some features of his story have been discredited.

that he saw the potential for his home town of being identified as the site of an extraordinary happening and wanted to keep the Roswell-UFO link in the news to encourage tourism. If so, it certainly worked, but in truth his motives will never be known.

Kaufmann's story was accepted as true by researchers for more than a decade. It also had a profound impact on how a great many researchers and members of the public envisaged the events of July 1947 unfolding. It is worth repeating that the main claims made by Kaufmann cannot be substantiated elsewhere and so must be considered to be untrue. It

will be seen that once these are stripped out of the Roswell story, some major gaps in the supposed chronology of the events will open up. These need not necessarily invalidate the entire Roswell story, but they do put a different slant on how events should be viewed.

According to Kaufmann/Osborn/Mac-Kenzie he was called in to Roswell on 2 July to help follow by radar some very strange and unidentified flying objects that were being tracked over New Mexico. Having reported to Roswell, he was sent to White Sands where the radar team was short-handed. At the end of a long shift, nothing much had happened other

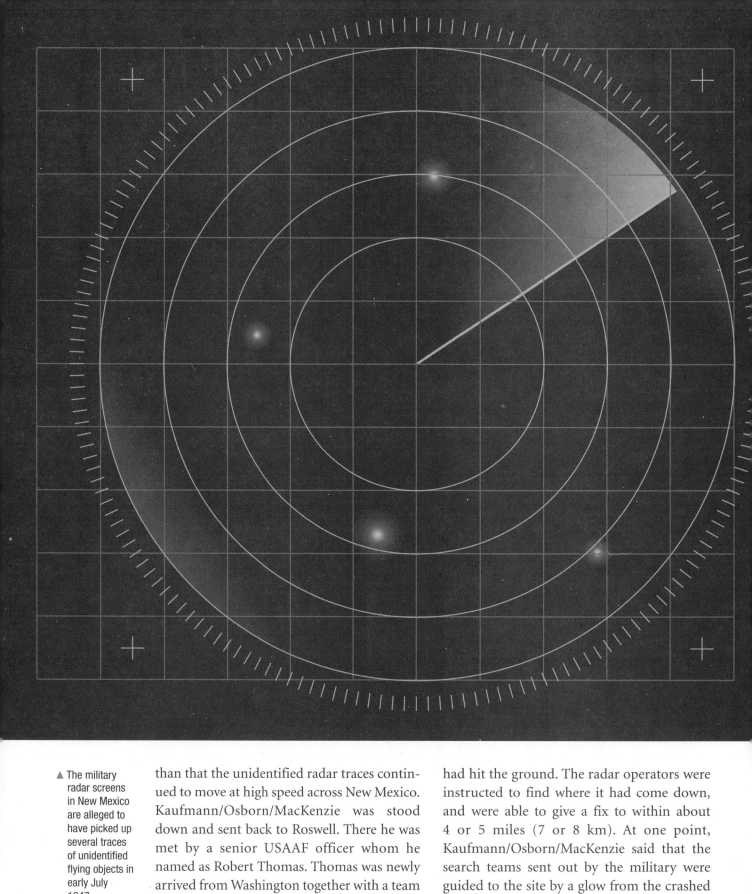

▲ The military radar screens in New Mexico are alleged to have picked up several traces of unidentified flying objects in early July 1947.

than that the unidentified radar traces continued to move at high speed across New Mexico. Kaufmann/Osborn/MacKenzie was stood down and sent back to Roswell. There he was met by a senior USAAF officer whom he named as Robert Thomas. Thomas was newly arrived from Washington together with a team of specialists and a lorry load of equipment.

According to Kaufmann/Osborn/Mac-Kenzie he returned to radar duties at Roswell on the evening of 4 July. At 11.20 pm one of the mysterious radar traces began to move erratically, then flared up before vanishing completely. It was assumed that the object

had hit the ground. The radar operators were instructed to find where it had come down, and were able to give a fix to within about 4 or 5 miles (7 or 8 km). At one point, Kaufmann/Osborn/MacKenzie said that the search teams sent out by the military were guided to the site by a glow from the crashed UFO, which would seem to indicate that they found the wreckage at night. He later said that the search teams did not find the crashed saucer until an hour or so after dawn, and that unauthorized civilians were on the site by then.

The account given by Kaufmann/Osborn/

MacKenzie indicates that a high-level team of senior officers moved in very quickly to take over control of the Crash Site. He named some of the men given access to the site, of whom some can be identified and some cannot. Among those known from other sources to be in Roswell at the time were William Blanchard, commander of the Roswell air base, Edwin Easley, the head of the military police on the base, and Oliver 'Pappy' Henderson, a senior pilot. Those known only from Kaufmann/ Osborn/MacKenzie's account include more shadowy figures such as Howard Fletcher and Lucas.

Again according to Kaufmann/Osborn/ MacKenzie, the clear-up operation at the Crash Site took several days. The bodies of the dead aliens and the remnants of their spacecraft were transported by truck back to Roswell air base. There they were placed in Hangar 84 and kept under armed guard. After the senior officers were certain that everything had been recovered from the Crash Site, the remains were crated up ready to be flown out to Wright Air Field for study. It was at this point that Brazel made his report. Thereafter the accounts given by Kaufmann/Osborn/ MacKenzie follow what is known from other sources.

It can be seen that the version of events given by Kaufmann/Osborn/MacKenzie filled in the crucial gap between the crash and the events that followed Brazel arriving in Sheriff Wilcox's office. It was Kaufmann/Osborn/ MacKenzie who claimed that the USAAF had been plotting the UFO by radar and had detected its crash. It was he who mentioned a team of high-ranking officers arriving from Washington DC and it was he who stated that the wreckage was stored at Roswell air base amid high security before being flown out. If the story told by Kaufmann/Osborn/ MacKenzie is discarded, then much of the evidence linking the Crash Site to the Debris Field is lost. Unfortunately, once that link had

▲ Pappy Henderson has been named by some witnesses as one of the few men given access to the Crash Site, but his accounts do not match up.

been firmly established, many researchers continued to work on the assumption that the two were linked, even after Kaufmann was unmasked.

GLENN DENNIS' TESTIMONY

In part the link between the two was maintained, and is maintained, by the testimony of Glenn Dennis. The evidence given by Dennis is usually considered to fall into two categories. The 'early version' is that sequence of events recounted by Dennis to friends and family

▲ The notorious 'Hangar 84' at Roswell, in which the alien craft is alleged to have been stored while it was on the base.

before the Roswell case achieved great fame, and is consistent with the statements he made to early researchers. The 'late version' includes additional information and claims that Dennis recounted only much later, after the alleged Roswell crash had become newsworthy.

Some researchers believe Dennis to be a prime witness of honesty. Others are willing to accept the early version of Dennis' evidence, believing that it has added credibility since he was telling people about it before the case became famous. These researchers dismiss the late version on the grounds that Dennis volunteered this additional evidence only after the Roswell case became well known and he stood to earn money by giving interviews to the media. Sceptics refuse to accept any of Dennis' evidence as being true. They argue that since he changed his story, nothing of what he says can be trusted.

▲ Glenn Dennis gave testimony of the utmost importance, but in recent years some aspects of his story have been questioned by researchers.

It is probably best to take the early version of Dennis' story first. According to this the events that he recalled took place in the summer of 1947. At first he was unable to remember the date, but when researchers began interviewing him he claimed to be able to fix the date as being in June or July, but could not be any more precise.

He was certain that the events began at about 1.30 pm on a work day as he was eating his lunch at work when the phone rang. At that time, Dennis was 22 years old and working as an apprentice in the Ballard Funeral House in Roswell. Ballard's had a contract to provide emergency mortuary services for anyone who died on the air base, caring for the body until the next of kin could be contacted to make a decision about how the body should be treated. The Ballard staff – including Glenn Dennis – were therefore occasional visitors to the air base and were authorized to enter the outer compound.

According to Dennis, the phone call was from a medical officer on the air base who was Ballard's usual contact in cases of a fatality. The officer asked Dennis what was the smallest size of hermetically sealed casket that Ballard's had available. Dennis replied that they held in stock only adult-sized coffins but could get child-sized or even baby-sized caskets at 24 hours' notice if required. The officer thanked Dennis and then rang off.

About an hour later the same officer was back on the line. This time he wanted to know how Ballard's would go about treating a body that had been lying out in the desert for a few days and had begun to decompose. Dennis began to explain, but when he mentioned that some strong chemicals would usually be employed, the officer interrupted to ask if this would affect the chemical composition of the bodies. Dennis said it would, then offered to come out to the air base to advise on how to handle a body. The officer at once said that there was no body, and that he was asking

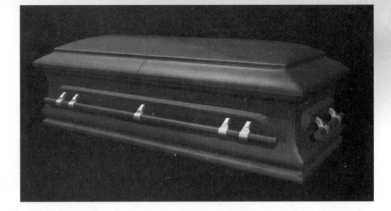

▲ A child-sized coffin of the type that Dennis says USAAF officers were asking about in July 1947.

these questions merely for future reference in case any such accident might happen.

Dennis says that there was something about the officer's behaviour and tone of voice that was distinctly odd. Dennis formed the opinion that a person had died either at or near the base several days earlier, but that the base was trying to keep the matter secret. The question about small caskets led him to surmise that children were involved. He thought that perhaps there had been an air crash nearby involving important civilians or high-ranking military personnel.

Dennis replied that they held in stock only adult-sized coffins but could get child-sized or even baby-sized caskets at 24 hours' notice if required.

One of the other services that Ballard's provided to the Roswell air base was to act as an ambulance service for non-emergency cases. Any serviceman or woman needing treatment that could not be provided by the medical teams on base would be ferried to Roswell hospital by Ballard's. Later that afternoon, Dennis recalled, he was sent to drive a USAAF-enlisted man from the hospital back to base. The job passed off without incident,

but things took a turn for the worse once he was on the base. Dennis accompanied the man into the sick bay area to complete his paperwork and then headed off to the staff lounge to get himself a drink.

On his way to the lounge, Dennis was stopped by a USAAF captain whom he did not recognize. The officer stopped Dennis and demanded to know who he was and what he was doing on the base. Dennis explained but the officer was clearly unimpressed. He called over two military policemen (MPs) and ordered them to escort Dennis back to his vehicle and off the air base.

THREATS

As Dennis was led away, a voice barked out, 'We're not through with that son of a bitch. Bring him back here.' The two MPs dragged Dennis back to face a second officer. He had red hair and again Dennis did not recognize him. According to Dennis, this new officer not only told him that he should not be on the base, but also to keep silent about anything he had seen or heard, especially with relevance to the requests for coffins. The officer concluded: 'If you say anything you could get into a lot of trouble.'

Dennis claims that he did not take well to the aggressive tone of the soldier, and responded: 'Hey look mister, I'm a civilian and you can't do a damn thing to me.' The officer glared back, then snarled, 'Yes we can. Somebody will be picking your bones out of the sand.' One of the MPs then chipped in with his own threat. 'He would make good dog food for our dogs.' That seems to have settled things and the rather shaken Dennis was escorted to his car by the two MPs, who then followed him until he was off the air base.

The following day Sheriff Wilcox called on Dennis' father, a friend of his, to warn him

that USAAF men had been in the sheriff's office asking questions about Dennis. Dennis' father assumed from this that his son was in some sort of trouble and gave the young man a warning to stay away from the air base for a while.

The day's events were certainly unusual. They made a great impression on Dennis, who repeated them to friends and relatives over the years. They do seem to have been out of the ordinary, but it is not immediately obvious how they are linked to the alleged UFO crash.

Most of the researchers into the Roswell Incident have decided that Dennis had inadvertently stumbled across the retrieval process. The phone calls demanding information about small coffins and how to treat bodies that had been out in the desert have been interpreted as being requests for caskets of the correct size for the 4 ft (1.2m) tall bodies reported by witnesses. The concern about how the chemicals would affect the composition of the bodies themselves has been interpreted as a worry over how preservatives might affect the alien bodies before they could be properly studied.

Dennis' encounter with the two aggressive military officers has been most often linked with Frank Kaufmann's claims that a team of specialists was brought in from Washington DC. The fact that Dennis did not recognize the pair might indicate that they were not usually based at Roswell. That neither officer seemed to be aware that civilians were allowed on the base, at least into the outer compound, is another indication that they were outsiders. Their hostility would indicate that they were both surprised and angered by the presence of a civilian.

This has usually been interpreted to imply that Dennis had stumbled on to a great secret of some kind – by implication the presence of alien bodies and a crashed UFO. However, this need not be the case. If the two officers were from elsewhere they may well have been simply concerned that a civilian was apparently wandering around the base of the world's only atomic bomber squadron. The conversation with the sheriff had, apparently, involved questions aimed at discovering if Dennis was a local man for whom the sheriff could vouch or a recent arrival to Roswell. Any spy interested in the bombers would most likely be from out of town. The questions may have been designed merely to establish this fact. Certainly the military did not pursue Dennis further.

The visit by military men to Wilcox to ask questions about Dennis would certainly indicate that there was a worry among the USAAF that Dennis had seen or heard something that they wanted to keep secret. It is important to note, however, that at the time of the incident

> **"**
> **There was a worry among the USAAF that Dennis had seen or heard something that they wanted to keep secret.**

itself Dennis does not seem to have been certain what it was he was supposed to have discovered. His reaction seems to have been more one of bewilderment and perplexity.

Although Dennis did not specify a date for what he saw, he was clear that it took place on a work day in June or July. Given the estimated sequence of events relating to the UFO crash, it would seem that Dennis' experiences took place after the UFO crash but before Brazel reported his finds. This would explain why the USAAF were so keen to enforce his silence.

If that was the case then the date of Dennis' unsettling encounter could only have been on 3, 4 or 5 July. Brazel reported his finds on Monday 7 July; the previous day was a Sunday so Dennis would not have been at work. If the crash occurred on the night of 4 July, then

Dennis must have been talking about 5 July. If the crash took place on the night of 2 July then he might have been referring to events on 3 or 4 July instead. Unfortunately no paperwork from Ballard's survives to show when Dennis was on duty.

REVISED ACCOUNT

So much for the early version given by Glenn Dennis. His later version of events is rather more dramatic. According to this account, Dennis had found a truck parked by the base hospital. Inside it he glimpsed some strange pieces of wreckage. These were shaped rather

like the bottom of a canoe and were about 3 ft (90 cm) long. They were of a dull, silvery colour with a sort of purplish sheen to them. At least one was marked by what seemed to be hieroglyphic markings or writing of some kind.

After dropping off the injured man, Dennis had not gone to look for a drink but to search for a friend of his. This friend was a nurse of about his own age who was a second lieutenant and had arrived at the base some three months earlier. Dennis says that he went into the base hospital to look for her.

As he strolled down a corridor, the nurse emerged from an examining room with a cloth clapped over her nose and mouth. She looked terrified. Seeing Dennis she blurted out, 'My gosh, get out of here or you're going to be in a lot of trouble.' It was at this point that the aggressive officers appeared and Dennis had his encounter with them.

The next day, according to Dennis' later account, he made contact with the nurse and arranged to meet her. The girl was still distressed, deeply so. She told Dennis that she had been asked to assist a doctor in a preliminary examination of a very strange body that had been brought in to the air base under conditions of great secrecy. 'This was something no one has ever seen,' the nurse told him.

▲ An artist's impression of the retrieval process at the Crash Site. The body of an alien is carried on a stretcher to a tent for preliminary examination, as men carry away the scattered pieces of wreckage.

According to the nurse, as relayed by Dennis, the body was one of three. Each body was a little less than 4 ft (1.2 m) tall and stank with the most appalling stench the nurse had ever experienced. The head of the corpse examined was larger in proportion to the body than that of a human, was entirely bald and the ears were so small as to be insignificant. The nose was tiny and little more than two small holes, while the mouth was more like a small slit than anything else and the teeth made of a soft material akin to cartilage. The arms ended in four fingers, each with

> **When he was first interviewed by researchers Dennis said that he had promised the nurse he would never reveal her identity.**

what seemed to be a small suction cup on its tip. Dennis said the nurse jotted down a few sketches of the bodies and body parts, but that he had lost them over the years. When interviewed by researchers he drew what he said were fairly close copies, but could not be certain how accurate they really were.

The nurse said that the supervising officers had insisted that the air conditioning be turned off so that the smell given off by the bodies did not permeate the entire building. However, this had made the stench in the examining room so horrific that she had fled – and it was at this point that she had met Dennis in the corridor. The bodies were subsequently moved to a large hangar for examination before being packed up and flown off the base.

Dennis claimed that a few days later the nurse vanished from Roswell. He found out that she had been transferred to a base in Britain, but thought it odd that she had gone without talking to him or leaving him a message. He wrote to her, but the letter was returned to him marked 'Return to sender – deceased'. He later heard a rumour that the girl had been killed in an aircraft crash along with five other nurses but was never able to confirm this. When he was first interviewed by researchers Dennis said that he had promised the nurse he would never reveal her identity. Nonetheless he did give the name Naomi Selff, which turned out to be false.

The fact that Dennis has never revealed the nurse's true name has been considered by some researchers to be another reason not to believe his later version of events. As we shall see, however, there was a nurse at Roswell who may have served as the basis for the person described by Dennis. And there may have been a very good reason for Dennis being cagey about her identity.

GOVERNOR'S VISIT

Another account of a visit to the base that occurred around the same date adds to the evidence that something very odd was going on at Roswell air base. Pete Anaya was, in 1947, one of several civilian workers who went on to the air base to undertake various manual tasks. Because he had a car and was a Spanish speaker Anaya was sometimes asked to drive Hispanic visitors, including Joseph Montoya, the Governor of New Mexico. Pete and his brother Ruben had got to know the governor reasonably well due to his visits to Roswell.

One afternoon in the summer of 1947 (neither Anaya brother can date it more precisely), Governor Montoya came to Roswell and asked the brothers to drive him out to the Roswell air base. Once through the main gate, Montoya directed Pete to pull up outside a hangar where a nurse and some other personnel were waiting. There were several military police officers who came to stand by the car, stopping Pete Anaya from taking more than a few steps. The governor climbed out of the car and walked into the hangar. When

Montoya came out again a while later he was looking pale and shocked. The nurse followed him out and said something to him as he was about to get back into the car.

Montoya slumped into the seat declaring, 'Get me the hell out of here. Quick.' As they left the base he insisted on being driven back to Pete's house for a drink. The Anayas recall him drinking neat whisky, which was very unlike him, and babbling on about small men with big heads. One of the men had been alive and moving. He also talked at length about a strange flying craft that 'moved like a platter and flies without wings'.

Research has shown that the only date in July that Governor Montoya visited Roswell was 7 July 1947. It is not certain that the Anaya brothers were referring to this particular visit as they could not recall the date, and Montoya was a fairly frequent visitor to the area. However, the date of 7 July does corre-late with the known date of the Roswell Incident. Those investigating the alleged saucer crash usually ascribe the visit described by the Anayas as being this one.

The evidence relating to the retrieval of a wrecked flying saucer from the Crash Site was all collected more than thirty years after the event, in some cases forty years. Although some of the evidence is at face value highly dramatic and certainly indicates that a flying machine of unknown construction and origin did crash, that evidence is all controversial to some extent or another. The same could not be said of the evidence relating to the retrieval of wreckage from the Debris Field. Most of that evidence is contemporary with the events described, or comes from witnesses of unimpeachable honesty.

All of which would make the retrieval at the Debris Field, if anything, even more controversial.

▲ Governor Montoya was a well-known figure in New Mexico in 1947. His visit to the air base is potentially a crucial piece of evidence, but it cannot be precisely dated.

5

The Debris
Field Retrieval

WHEN RANCHER Mac Brazel walked into the office of Chaves County Sheriff George Wilcox some time late in the morning of 7 July neither man could have had any idea of what events were about to unfold. Wilcox was later to say that if he had known what was going to happen over the next few days he would have handled matters very differently. Brazel would soon be of the same opinion. But neither man knew then what they would realize later, so events unfolded as they did.

At first the rancher, in his old clothes, came in to report some odd debris on his land and was dealt with by a deputy. But when the deputy saw the debris in the box he called Wilcox over. Wilcox fiddled with the strange pieces of what seemed to be metal and fabric and asked Brazel a few questions. Brazel seemed to Wilcox keen both to report what he feared may have been an aircraft accident of some kind, and to have somebody come and clear the rubbish off his land. Wilcox called Roswell air base, suspecting that if anything odd fell out of the sky then it was most likely to be something to do with the secretive USAAF bases in the area.

was a usual routine for Joyce, who called most days to ask if anything newsworthy had happened that he could pass on as a matter of public information or as an interesting anecdote to liven up his programme. Still not taking Brazel and his debris very seriously, Wilcox passed the phone to the rancher. Brazel and Joyce had a quick chat that resulted in Joyce broadcasting a short item about a mysterious crash of strange debris taking place near Roswell.

In hindsight, this small incident would come to assume great importance. If those who believe that an alien spacecraft did crash at Roswell are correct then Joyce's short news item was the catalyst for everything that would follow. Up to this point, the USAAF had managed to keep a tight lid on the crash and had stopped news leaking out. Barnett, Holden and others who had seen the Crash Site had been effectively silenced. The area around the Crash Site had been cordoned off by armed guards. Everything had seemed to be under control. But now news was out. As we shall see later it is alleged that it was at this point that a highly complex and effective cover-up began.

▶ A radio of 1940s vintage. In rural areas of the USA in 1947, local radio stations played an important role in keeping their communities informed of local events.

FIRST BROADCAST

A few minutes later Frank Joyce, the announcer and news reporter for local radio station KGFL, called the sheriff's office. This

▲ Frank Joyce spoke to rancher Brazel the day he reported his find of debris.

Meanwhile, the developing chain of events was dragging more and more men into the Roswell Incident. The next man to be involved was Major Jesse Marcel, head of intelligence at Roswell air base.

As the research into the Roswell Incident and its chronology developed, there appeared some discrepancies in the testimony of Marcel. The most serious of these related to how quickly he reacted to the phone call from Wilcox alerting him to Brazel's arrival. In the earlier accounts produced in the 1980s, it is reported that Brazel went into Wilcox's office late on the morning of Monday 7 July. Wilcox phoned Marcel at lunchtime and Marcel drove out to Brazel's ranch that afternoon to inspect the wreckage. By the 1990s the chronology had changed to make Brazel's visit to Wilcox take place on Sunday 6 July. Marcel was phoned at lunchtime, but did not get out to Brazel's ranch until the evening by which time it was too dark to see anything. He therefore stayed the night with Brazel, setting out to inspect the Debris Field on the morning of 7 July.

Both versions have Marcel being shown the Debris Field by Brazel on Monday 7 July. Bill Brazel, Mac's elder son, recalls that his father went into Roswell to do some business and that the trip to see Wilcox was incidental. Clearly no business could have been done in Roswell on a Sunday in 1947, so this would seem to indicate that Brazel visited Wilcox on the Monday. The discrepancy between the different chronologies given by Marcel has never been satisfactorily explained.

INSPECTING THE DEBRIS FIELD

Whenever Marcel headed out to the Foster Ranch to meet Brazel, it is clear that the inspection of the Debris Field took place on the afternoon of Monday 7 July. Marcel arrived at the Foster Ranch in a saloon car. Following him in a jeep was a junior intelligence officer, Sheridan Cavitt, who would later rise to the rank of lieutenant colonel. Brazel had saddled up horses for all three men as the Debris Field lay a few miles away over land quite unsuitable for a road car. However, Marcel had never ridden a horse. He was unwilling to make his first ride over broken country on a mount accustomed only to experienced horsemen. Brazel rode out,

◄ An off-road vehicle crosses the New Mexico desert. Access to the Debris Field by Marcel and other USAAF personnel was in this type of vehicle.

followed by Marcel and Cavitt in the jeep.

Marcel recalled the Debris Field was about 1,000 yd (915 m) long and about 200 ft (60 m) wide. The pieces of debris were mostly fairly small, the largest being a yard or so across. They were hung up on bushes and fluttered in the breeze. Marcel's description of the debris matched that given by other witnesses – it was light but incredibly strong, and returned to its original shape when folded or crumpled up. Marcel's immediate impression, which he never changed, was that something had exploded in the air high above, sending debris showering down to the ground.

Cavitt, like Marcel, was still alive when researchers began delving into the events at Roswell in the 1980s. Unlike Marcel, however,

Marcel's description of the debris matched that given by other witnesses – it was light but incredibly strong, and returned to its original shape when folded or crumpled up.

he was still serving with the military and had risen high in the ranks of the highly secretive counter intelligence services. Unsurprisingly, he was reluctant to talk to civilian investigators and soon acquired a reputation for being tight-lipped and evasive about his role at Roswell in 1947. Some suspected that he had been actively involved in the cover-up that some alleged had been taking place. Under this scenario, Cavitt was thought to have been fully aware of the Crash Site and what was going on there at the time that he and Marcel went to the Foster Ranch. It is alleged that Cavitt was sent along to keep an eye on Marcel and to ensure that as little as possible of the real situation leaked out.

When he eventually agreed to be inter-

viewed in May 1994, Cavitt insisted that before he said anything he should be given written clearance from the Secretary of the Air Force to discuss classified information with the interviewer. Once this had been obtained, Cavitt was interviewed.

Generally his evidence agreed with that given by Marcel, though Cavitt recalled that they had gone out to the Foster Ranch on 8 July, and not on the evening of 7 July. His recollections diverge from Marcel's principally over the description of the debris that the two men found. Cavitt recalled that it consisted of four distinct types. The first he said was a thin metal foil that he took to be aluminium sheeting of some kind. He described this as being very lightweight and thin, but did not think it was particularly unusual and certainly did not recall the incredible strength ascribed to it by others. He also remembered some short sections of wooden or bamboo splints about half an inch (13 mm) across and 3 inches (75 mm) long. He was quite certain that these were wooden in nature. He also recalled a much larger quantity of a darker, plastic-like sheeting, of which the vast bulk of the debris was composed. Again, he recalled nothing very special about this sheeting except that it was tattered and torn into hundreds of fragments. There was also, he recalled, a lightweight box that seemed to be sealed shut and which he made no attempt to open.

Asked what he had thought at the time, Cavitt replied without hesitation that he believed that they had found a high altitude balloon of some kind, together with its payload. Cavitt was clear and unequivocal in his recollections. Taken at face value they completely demolished the idea that an alien spacecraft had crashed at Roswell. However, researchers quickly pointed out that Cavitt was a senior intelligence officer who might have reasons to give an officially authorized version of events. His evidence, in any case, related solely to the Debris Field, not to the Crash Site.

Whatever the nature of the debris found, both Cavitt and Marcel agree about what they did with it. Large quantities were collected and thrown into the back of the jeep. When the jeep was full, Marcel ordered Cavitt to drive it back to the air base. Cavitt did so, depositing the debris in Marcel's office. Marcel stayed on the Debris Field to collect what he considered to be the more interesting pieces of what remained. This he loaded into the saloon car.

As the sun set Marcel drove away from the Foster Ranch. On his way back to the base he stopped off at his home. There, Marcel woke his 11-year-old son, Jesse Junior, so that he could show the debris to him as well as to his wife. Jesse Junior was interviewed several times by researchers and claimed to recall the night's activities clearly.

He said that his father brought a box of debris into the house from the car. The box was emptied on to the kitchen floor, almost filling the space available. They made some attempts to fit the fragments together as if working on a jigsaw puzzle, but soon gave the task up as impossible. Like his father and others, he recalled that the metal sheeting was both lightweight and incredibly strong, while the small struts would not catch fire and were likewise of great strength. He recalled the purplish markings resembling geometric shapes and circles on the struts. Marcel's son also recalled the darker, plastic-like sheeting and again thought that it had been incredibly

▲ Pieces of debris spread out on the kitchen floor of the Marcel house, as recalled by Jesse Marcel Junior speaking some years after the events.

strong and impossible to tear. Having shown his family the box of strange wreckage, Marcel continued on to the Roswell air base.

Having shown the officer the location of the Debris Field, Mac Brazel rode off to get on with his work. At some time in the later afternoon he returned to his ranch house. There

> According to Bill Brazel, Mac's son, an entire platoon of men moved on to the Foster Ranch on 8 or 9 July and stayed for a day or two.

he met Walt Whitmore, the owner of the KGFL radio station, who had come out to ask for an interview. The ranch did not have a phone, which was why Whitmore had driven. The move shows that Whitmore was well aware of the news value of the apparent capture of a flying saucer even this early in the unfolding story.

BRAZEL INTERVIEWED

Brazel agreed to give an interview, and was driven back to the KGFL studios in Roswell by Whitmore. They recorded the interview, but by the time they had finished it was too late to broadcast it as KGFL went off the air at 10 pm each night – not at all unusual for local radio stations in the 1940s. It was also too late for Whitmore to drive Brazel home, so the rancher stayed overnight at Whitmore's house.

Next morning, 8 July, it became clear that Whitmore was not the only one taking the story seriously. A USAAF officer from Roswell air base, presumably alerted to Brazel's visit to Whitmore by Marcel or Cavitt, arrived to invite the rancher to travel to the air base to help the air force with some questions. Once again, Brazel was happy to go though he must by this time have been beginning to

wonder when he would get back to his ranch. It would be longer than he could possibly have imagined.

Exactly where Brazel went and what he did over the next few days has long been a subject of some controversy. He certainly spent most of that day at the Roswell air base. He seems to have been questioned by intelligence officers, but not by Marcel, and was lodged in the comfortable guest house that was on the base for the use of visiting dignitaries. So far as can be deduced he was not held under duress but neither was he allowed to go home. Brazel would not reappear in public without a military escort for some days.

Meanwhile, Marcel and Cavitt were back at Roswell air base. On the morning of 8 July, Marcel went to see the base commander, Colonel William Blanchard. Blanchard, according to Marcel, questioned him briefly about the Debris Field and then poked about in one of the boxes of material that had been brought back to the base. Blanchard ordered Marcel to load the wreckage on to a B-29 aircraft and fly it to Wright air base for analysis. As was usual for transport flights out of Roswell, Marcel was to take a squadron aircraft to Fort Worth in Dallas from where he would transfer to the next aircraft available for the flight on to Ohio. Blanchard said that he would send out another team of men to the Foster Ranch to collect up the rest of the debris.

According to Bill Brazel, Mac's son, an entire platoon of men moved on to the Foster Ranch on 8 or 9 July and stayed for a day or two. He said that they 'picked up every piece and shred they could find'. The material was loaded on to trucks and taken back to Roswell air base.

HUNTING FOR DEBRIS

The men sent out by Blanchard were not the only ones looking for the Debris Field that day. When the press release announcing the crash of a flying saucer went out on the Associated Press (AP) wire it provoked a massive response. Among the first to move was the AP itself. It advised its many media clients that it was chasing the story and turned to its nearest staff reporter to do the job. That man was Jason Kellahin who was based in Albuquerque to cover New Mexico for the AP. Kellahin was instructed to drive down to Roswell to find out everything he could about the story. He was also told to take photos and send them back to the AP by wire. Kellahin knew that sending photos over telephone wires required some complex equipment and was not certain that he was competent to deal with the technical issues involved in sending photos from a small town like Roswell. He therefore took with him a technician named Robin Adair.

Interviewed in the 1980s, Kellahin said that he and Adair drove down the main road towards Roswell, stopping at Vaughn for a break. In Vaughn Kellahin asked around for information about Brazel and his ranch. He

encountered by Kellahin were the squad sent out by Blanchard to clear the Debris Field.

This part of Kellahin's statement has caused some controversy since. The site that is generally recognized as being the pasture where the Debris Field was located lies about 2 miles (3 km) from the nearest dirt road, and yet Kellahin says that he and Adair walked to the Debris Field in just a couple of minutes.

Some have suggested that the military had deliberately constructed a false 'debris field' close to the road to mislead any snooping journalists – such as Kellahin. Others have sought to use the discrepancy to discredit Kellahin as a witness, implying that if he was mistaken about this point then his memory cannot be trusted on other matters. Of course, it may be that after forty years, Kellahin's memory was slightly at fault at this point. Perhaps he saw the military vehicles parked at the side of the road but the Debris Field was some distance away. Perhaps the vehicles were a mile or more off the road, but he was able to drive his road car some dis-

◀ The main road north of Roswell along which witnesses were driving when they saw military personnel in the desert.

was given directions on how to reach the ranch house by driving down Highway 285, then turning off along dirt roads. Kellahin followed the directions, but before he actually reached the ranch he saw a group of military vehicles parked in open country with some men standing around them. Assuming that this military activity marked the location where Brazel had found the Debris Field, Kellahin stopped his car and with Adair walked over the rough ground to join the men. It is generally believed that these men

tance over the pasture so that his walk was as short as he believed.

Whatever the truth about the location of the military vehicles, Kellahin says that he and Adair reached them on foot to find a handful of officers, a larger number of enlisted men and one civilian. The civilian turned out to be Mac Brazel, one of the men the AP had instructed Kellahin to interview. Whipping out his notebook, Kellahin got on with the job unhindered by the military men. So far as Kellahin could recall, Brazel repeated the facts about finding the debris, reporting it to Sheriff Wilcox and assisting the military in the retrieval operation.

While the interview was going on, Adair was photographing the enlisted men at work. They were collecting pieces of debris and loading it on to trucks. Kellahin recalled that the pieces were all fairly small. He said that they were of two types: firstly, a silver-coloured foil material and secondly, what looked like narrow wooden sticks. One officer asked Kellahin not to touch the debris, so he did not. He thought that the debris covered a fairly small area; he estimated it as about

> ## The officers refused to talk to Kellahin, saying that they knew very little about the affair except that they had been ordered to collect the pieces of debris.

100 yd (80 m) or so. Asked what he thought the debris had come from, Kellahin said: 'It looked more like a kite than anything else.'

When Kellahin finished speaking to Brazel he tried to interview a couple of the officers. They refused to talk to him, saying that they knew very little about the affair except that they had been ordered to collect the pieces of debris lying about. Then one officer announced that they were finished on the ranch and had to head into Roswell.

Kellahin recalls staying behind on the site for a while after Brazel and the military men had gone. There was, he said, not much to see. The bits and pieces of debris had all been picked up, leaving behind just grass and scrub. Adair recalled it differently. Also speaking some forty years after the event, Adair said that 'you could tell something had been there'. These signs included scorched shrubs and burned grass. There were also a number of marks in the ground as if something large and

heavy had touched down briefly. Perhaps a flying object had come down at speed and then glanced off the ground to bounce back into the air. Whatever the state of the ground, Kellahin and Adair did not stay long but headed into Roswell to continue their assignment.

It took until about 3 pm on 8 July for Marcel to get an aircraft ready for his flight. Memories differ as to how much wreckage he took with him. Marcel recalled that there was 'half a B-29 full of the stuff.' However, one of the crew, Sergeant Robert Porter, recalled in the 1980s that there had been only four boxes of material. The largest of these had been about a yard (90 cm) across, while the others were barely a foot (30 cm) long.

DEBRIS FLOWN TO FORT WORTH

By the time Marcel took off, the crucial press release announcing to the world that a flying saucer had been captured had already been issued. We shall deal with the press release later when we look at the alleged cover-up, but for now what is important is that the press, but not the public, were aware of Marcel's mission before he took off. Also kept informed was General Roger Ramey, the commander of the US 8th Air Force which covered the Roswell air base. Ramey was based in Fort Worth and it seems likely that he had a conversation with Blanchard by phone before Marcel arrived. At any rate he knew all about the alleged flying saucer crash and Marcel's mission when the B-29 landed at Fort Worth.

As soon as the B-29 landed, a message came through that Marcel was to report to Ramey's office, taking with him some of the debris. The crew of the aircraft were ordered to stay with their plane until an armed guard arrived to take over from them – in the meantime nobody was to be allowed on to the aircraft. These orders were unusual, but not ridiculously so. On routine flights from Roswell to

Fort Worth the crew were allowed to disembark as soon as they had taxied to the allotted parking space and completed their end-of-flight checks. Any valuable cargo, however, would mean that the aircraft would not be allowed to stand alone at any time. Clearly, at this point, Ramey was treating the material on board as if it were of great value. When the armed guard arrived, Porter says that he and the rest of the crew wandered over to the mess to get something to eat and await further orders.

Marcel, meanwhile, was escorted to Ramey's office carrying a box of the debris. According to Marcel, he was asked to put the box down on Ramey's desk. The general took little apparent interest in the debris other than to glance at it. Instead he questioned Marcel about the circumstances of the find and where it had taken place. Ramey then called in Major Charles Cashon, the official public information officer for the Fort Worth air base. According to Marcel's first version of events, Cashon took one photo of him with

▲ Scorched grass and other vegetation is often reported to occur at UFO landing sites, and was reported as being present at the Debris Field.

the debris at this point. In his later accounts, Marcel placed the taking of this photo later.

Ramey then told Marcel that a group of newspaper and radio reporters were waiting outside the room to be let in. He told Marcel that he had to remain silent unless he was called upon by Ramey himself to answer a question. Ramey then asked Cashon to start unpacking the contents of the box. Marcel was beckoned out of the room to another chamber in which various maps of the Roswell area were laid out. Ramey insisted on being shown the exact place where the debris had been found. This took several minutes.

FAKE DEBRIS?

Ramey then led Marcel back to his office where Cashon was leaning on the desk with debris laid out on the floor around him. Marcel says that he realized at once that something was wrong. The debris on the floor was not the same material as that which he had brought into the room a few minutes earlier. Cashon then identified the material as having come from an ordinary weather balloon and not from a flying saucer. Marcel says that he protested that it was not the correct debris and bent down to look at it

"Newton arrived in Ramey's office a few minutes later, took one look at the debris and pronounced it to be a badly damaged weather balloon.

more closely. According to his later version of events, it was at this point that Cashon took a photo of Marcel with the debris.

The difference in Marcel's versions is crucial as a photo that is thought to be that taken by Cashon has survived. According to

Marcel's first version this photo should show the real debris collected from the Foster Ranch, but in his second version it would show the fake debris. The photo shows Marcel squatting down on his haunches with a pair of wooden chairs behind him. He is looking up to a person out of shot to the left while in his hands he holds what looks like a thin sheet of metal about 18 inches (450 mm) or so across. Even those who maintain that the wreckage was incredibly strong and virtually indestructible say that it looked very similar to ordinary aluminium foil. From the photo alone it is impossible to tell if the object Marcel is holding is normal foil or alien metal.

According to Marcel, while he was protesting to Cashon about the apparent switch of material, Ramey was on the phone demanding somebody come over to his office. This person later turned out to be Warrant Officer Irving Newton, the Fort Worth meteorologist. In the course of his duties Newton would have handled dozens of weather balloons both before they were launched and after they were retrieved. He could have been relied upon to recognize a weather balloon no matter how badly damaged it had been in a crash or when left blowing in the wind around the desert scrub.

Newton arrived in Ramey's office a few minutes later, took one look at the debris and pronounced it to be a badly damaged weather balloon. He guessed that it had been lying in the open for some days judging by the effect of wind and sun on the material. Marcel says that he continued to protest that the objects shown to Newton were not part of the original debris, but that he was ordered to shut up by Ramey.

When he was interviewed in the 1990s, Newton – by then a major – recalled the events rather differently. Like Marcel, he was speaking decades after the event, but also like Marcel he insisted that he recalled the events clearly. According to Newton he had been on duty alone in the weather centre at Fort Worth air base when his phone rang. On the line was an officer on Ramey's staff who asked Newton to come over to the general's office for a few minutes. Newton's office was some distance away from Ramey's across the vast air base and he was on duty on his own. Newton explained to the officer that he could not leave the weather centre unmanned and so could not comply. The officer rang off.

A few seconds later Ramey himself was on the line. He ordered Newton to come over to his office at once, telling him to commandeer a car to get there quicker if he had to. Once again, Newton began to explain that he was on duty alone but Ramey cut in to tell him in no uncertain terms: 'Get your ass over here. Now!' Newton obliged.

When he arrived at the headquarters building, Newton was met by Colonel Thomas DuBose, Ramey's aide-de-camp (ADC). In answer to Newton's question as to what the fuss was about, the colonel told him that the Roswell air base had sent over some wreckage claiming that it may have come from a flying saucer but that Ramey thought it was a weather balloon. 'He wants you to take a look at it,' Newton was told.

Newton says that he was ushered into Ramey's office to find a mass of debris spread over the floor and desk. Newton recalled: 'As soon as I saw it I told them that this was a balloon and a Rawin target.'

Thus far his account matches that of Marcel, but Newton claimed that Marcel was angry and annoyed. According to Newton, Marcel was not angry that the material had been switched but that nobody believed it to be parts of a flying saucer. Newton recalls Marcel picking up pieces of the debris and forcing it into Newton's hands, telling him that the material was not of earthly origins and had to come from an alien spaceship. At one point, Newton says, Marcel picked up a strut that had purple markings on it and

▲ General Ramey almost certainly removed some of the wreckage before allowing journalists to enter his office.

insisted that the marks were alien hieroglyphs. Newton is adamant that they were simply abstract flowers, triangles and circles.

Newton then says that Ramey interrupted to ask him if he was absolutely certain that the debris on the floor came from a weather balloon. Newton says he replied, 'Hell, yes. I'm sure. I know what that is. That's a Rawin target and balloon and if it isn't I'd eat it without salt or pepper.'

Ramey photographed in his office with what he claimed was the wreckage brought in from Roswell.

◄ Jesse Marcel photographed in Ramey's office with the wreckage. Marcel was not allowed to speak to reporters at the time, but later claimed that the wreckage shown here was not the same as the debris he had brought from Roswell.

Both Newton and Marcel agree that the objects seen by Newton came from a weather balloon. The issue here is whether or not the material shown to Newton was the same as that brought from Roswell by Marcel. According to Marcel's account given some years later it had been switched, but Newton's version indicates that Marcel did not think at the time that a substitution had taken place.

PRESS CONFERENCE

Whatever the truth, it was at this point that the press conference took place at which Ramey announced that the alleged flying saucer was a crashed weather balloon. The press were allowed to photograph the debris in Ramey's office, along with Ramey and his staff. Newton was called upon to point out

▶ Lt Newton points out to reporters the distinguishing features of a weather balloon to be found on the wreckage displayed in Ramey's office.

the features of the debris that identified it as a weather balloon. Marcel was not allowed to say anything. After the conference, Ramey told Marcel that he was relieved of all responsibility for the debris and advised him to return to Roswell. Marcel rounded up Porter and the rest of the crew and did exactly that.

So far as Marcel was concerned that was the end of his involvement with the wreckage from the Debris Field. He felt aggrieved at the way he had been treated by Ramey and both puzzled and worried by the switch of the real debris for a torn weather balloon.

Marcel says that he was convinced then, and remained convinced ever afterwards, that a large scale cover-up was underway. The USAAF did not want the truth about the Roswell Incident to come out.

He was right. And they succeeded.

▲ Ramey (left) pieces together bits of the wreckage in his office to show reporters that it came from a weather balloon.

6

The
Cover-Up

THERE IS NO DOUBT at all that the USAAF launched a concerted and determined campaign to hide from the public the truth about what really happened in and around Roswell in early July 1947. The problem that researchers have been faced with is finding out what the truth was that was hidden so effectively.

So far as the press and public were aware in July 1947, the first overt sign that the USAAF was making a concerted effort to kill the story came with Ramey's press conference at which the general announced that the 'flying saucer' was really a weather balloon. Ramey later went on to a local radio station to repeat the story, ensuring that his message was recorded and passed on to radio stations nationwide for them to broadcast either the whole statement or parts of it on their news bulletins.

If that was the first move in the cover-up, it was far from being the last. Marcel and other serving military men were given orders never to talk about the incident again. Subject to military discipline as they were, these men could probably be counted on to keep quiet. But civilians had been involved and that meant that there were a lot of loose ends to be tied up.

There was, for instance, Mac Brazel, the rancher who had found the Debris Field in the first place. As witnessed by Kellahin, Brazel was taken on the afternoon of 8 July out to the Debris Field to ensure that the mil-

itary had picked up everything from the ranch. Brazel was then driven by his military escort to the offices of the *Roswell Daily Record*. The newspaper had in that day's edition printed the sensational story about a captured flying saucer. Now Ramey had issued his story that the 'saucer' was a crashed weather balloon and it was essential that the newspaper printed both Ramey's version and an update from Brazel that tied in with this.

BRAZEL UNDER ESCORT

Arriving at the offices of the *Roswell Daily Record*, Brazel was escorted in by two officers. Talking to the reporters, Brazel gave an interview that resulted in an article being printed the following day. In this version Brazel said that he had first seen the debris on 14 June when he had been out riding the ranch with his wife and two younger children, but that he had not investigated it closely until early July. The Debris Field was, he said, small and confined, being less than 200 yd (180 m) across. He said that he accepted the official explanation that the debris had come from a balloon, although it was unlike that from a weather balloon he had found some time earlier.

As he was leaving the newspaper office, Brazel passed two men he knew, Bill Jenkins and Leonard Porter. Although the two men said hello, Brazel ignored them and pushed past. The two men thought that this was as odd as the military escort their rancher friend

► The sign outside the offices of the *Roswell Daily Record*, the newspaper that first broke the story of the UFO crash and then quashed it by printing the explanations given by the USAAF.

had in tow. The incident certainly shows that Brazel's mind was preoccupied and is thought by some to indicate that he was acting under duress.

Brazel was then driven to the studios of the KGFL radio station. Whitmore was absent, but Frank Joyce was manning the desk. There Brazel repeated the story that he had told at the *Roswell Daily Record*. Joyce had heard the original version of the story given by Brazel to KGFL and recognized that this new account differed in some key respects. Recalling the incident years later, Joyce said that he pointed out the discrepancies to Brazel, but that the rancher insisted that the new story was the truth. He had then glanced towards his military escort and muttered something about how 'things could go hard for me' if he did not stick to the story. Then he had left.

Where Brazel went next and what happened to him is unclear. Bill Brazel, Mac's adult son, says that he saw his father's photo in his local newspaper alongside the report of a crashed saucer. Concerned that his father might need some help, Bill drove down to the Foster Ranch a couple of days later to find the place deserted. Knowing what needed doing around a ranch, Bill set to work, but by Monday 14 July his father had still not turned up and he began to worry. He drove to Corona and phoned Sheriff Wilcox, who had been named in the newspaper report as the person to whom Mac Brazel had reported his find. Bill Brazel was told that his father was fine and would be allowed home in a day or two. No reason was given as to why he was being held.

When Mac Brazel arrived back on the ranch he was little more communicative. Bill remembered his father saying, 'Gosh, I just tried to do a good deed and they put me in jail for it.' Bill was also told that the less he knew the better because 'that way nobody will bother you about it'. He got the impression that his father was upset and annoyed by the

way he had been treated by the USAAF. Nevertheless, Mac Brazel said that he had been told that what he had seen and heard related to national security and that he had been instructed not to discuss it. For the rest

▲ Was Brazel held in custody so that the USAAF could pressure him into colluding with them?

of his life, Mac Brazel said very little about what had happened. It can only be surmised that he was kept on Roswell air base for the week or so before he was allowed home. Perhaps he was questioned, perhaps not.

VISITS FROM THE MILITARY

Another man who was in a position to know what had really happened was Sheriff George Wilcox. He was visited by a pair of military officers who told him that they had come to take away the box of debris that Mac Brazel had brought in. Wilcox had kept the box locked up and was only too happy to hand it over. The officers then told Wilcox that the entire matter was one of national security and that he must not discuss it with anyone. If he received any inquiries from press or public then he should say nothing other than to pass the caller on to the USAAF. They told Wilcox that there would be 'grave consequences' if he did not comply.

According to Wilcox's wife, Inez, there was a second visit from the military a couple of weeks later. This visit was altogether more sinister. Wilcox was told bluntly that he would be killed if he spoke of the matter to the press.

> **For the rest of his life, Mac Brazel said very little about what had happened.**

Wilcox's staff recall that he seemed to lose interest in his job soon after the Roswell Incident. He did not run for re-election.

Dan Dwyer (the firefighter) and his daughter were visited and threatened. So was Herbert Ellis, a civilian contractor who had been working on Roswell air base at the time. It is not known what Ellis had seen, but several of his friends remembered the visit from military men who told him to keep quiet and issued threats. Walter Whitmore,

the owner of radio station KGFL, received a phone call from the authorities in Washington telling him that his company's licence to broadcast would be cancelled unless he dropped the story.

FIRST PRESS RELEASE

Another loose end was the press release issued by Lieutenant Walter Haut announcing the capture of a flying saucer. Several newspapers from 1947 report that Haut (he is sometimes named as 'Haught' as that was the spelling of his name given in the original AP wire story) received a rebuke direct from the Pentagon for having put out a press release and was ordered to retrieve it. Speaking in 1989, Haut denied that he had gone around the media in Roswell confiscating the original press release. Surviving staff from the newspapers and KPFG radio station do remember military officers calling round in the days after the original reports to ask for the return of the press release, but do not recall that it was Haut himself. In any case no original copy of that crucial first press release can be found today. There is only the AP wire story that was based upon it and the first report in the *Roswell Daily Record* that was likewise based on the release.

It is that vanished press release that brings us back to the issue of a cover-up and what exactly it was that was being covered up. It was the press release that sparked the media storm that was to engulf Roswell and the USAAF, and which General Ramey calmed with his announcement that the 'flying saucer' was only a weather balloon. Without it the story may never have got out. Certainly at the time the USAAF could have ensured the silence of anyone who had seen or heard anything, as indeed they did. And without the contemporary press stories to supply corroboration it is unlikely that the researcher Stanton Friedman would have given much credence to Jesse Marcel's story told in 1978.

So why did the USAAF issue that first press release?

It was Walter Haut who issued the press release, delivering it by hand to the media in Roswell who then passed it on nationwide over the AP wire service. Haut recalled in the 1980s that he had been ordered to issue the release by Colonel Blanchard in a phone call he received at around 11 am on Tuesday 8 July. Haut could not recall whether Blanchard dictated the wording over the phone or if he simply told Haut what the release should say. Either way, Haut was clear that Blanchard had approved the final version before Haut set off to take it into town.

This at once raises the question of whether or not Blanchard was permitted by higher authority to issue the release. As commander of Roswell air base, Blanchard would have had full authority to issue any news about the base or its personnel. He would not, however, have been authorized to issue any news or views about the missions or equipment of 509th Bomber Group. He would most certainly not have been able to issue any information about the highly classified atomic weapons with which the unit was armed. An event that happened at Roswell air base, but which was not directly related to the atomic unit, would have fallen to Blanchard's discretion. If he believed it to be of only minor importance he would probably have felt that he had authority to talk about it. Anything more important would most likely have been referred up the chain of command to an officer senior enough to feel that he had authority to deal with it.

Even in July 1947, when the whole idea of UFOs was new to the world, the capture of a crashed flying saucer undoubtedly rated as a major piece of news. The reaction of the American and world press to the AP story confirms this. Blanchard was an experienced military officer who had been given his

command partly because of his ability to deal with the press and public in a sensitive manner. He must surely have known that the release of news of a captured flying saucer would cause a media frenzy, as it did. It seems bizarre that he could have authorized Haut's press release without referring it up the line of command.

Blanchard's immediate superior was General Ramey in Fort Worth. It is clear that Ramey knew all about the alleged captured

▲ Lt Walter Haut issued the press release announcing the capture of a flying disk on the instructions of Colonel Blanchard.

▶ Colonel Blanchard and Major Ramey knew each other well and met frequently to discuss military business. It is not so clear how closely they liaised with each other over the Roswell Incident.

saucer by the time Marcel arrived with the debris en route to Wright Field air base in Ohio. It is unlikely that Ramey had phoned Blanchard once the story went out on the AP wire as we know that all phone lines to the Roswell air base were jammed with incoming calls from reporters within minutes. It is more likely that Blanchard had phoned Ramey before Haut got into Roswell with the press release. Although that leaves open the question of whether Blanchard consulted Ramey

before or after Haut set off, it seems likely that Blanchard had called Ramey first.

Authorizing the press release was not the only odd thing that Blanchard did that day. He also went on leave. For a base commander to abandon his post for a holiday when the world's press were besieging the place, clamouring for news of an incident, is odd enough. That a military commander might leave when he thought that his men had captured a UFO is even more baffling. It is usually taken that

Blanchard did genuinely believe that his men had acquired parts of a flying saucer. Not only had he authorized Haut's press release, but he had sent Marcel off with some of the debris to the highly secretive Wright Field so that it could be analyzed.

While Blanchard was away for the next three weeks his post was taken by his deputy, Lieutenant Colonel Payne Jennings. Jennings had been alerted on Sunday 6 July that he would be filling in for Blanchard. This was rather short notice, but not suspiciously so. What it does show, however, is that Blanchard decided to take his leave only two or three days before he went. Again this is somewhat unusual, but not bizarre.

Given the timings of the various events relating to the Roswell Incident, however, the timing of Blanchard's leave takes on new importance. According to the official version put out by the USAAF, the first the military had known of anything unusual was when Sheriff Wilcox phoned Major Marcel on 7 July when Mac Brazel arrived in Roswell with his box of debris. Marcel had then gone out to collect the debris, returning to Roswell air base late that evening. He had then shown the debris to Blanchard on the morning of 8 July, whereupon Blanchard authorized the press release and went on leave.

Since it is very unlikely that Blanchard would have gone for a holiday when his base had captured a flying saucer, the official version seems unlikely to be true. Sceptics argue that Blanchard did not go on leave until after Ramey had unmasked the debris as being from a weather balloon. They point to a press report dated 9 July saying that Blanchard had gone on leave, but all this proves is that he had left by noon on 9 July, not that he was on the base until then. In any case, several of the military witnesses, including Haut, say that they remember Blanchard leaving before Ramey's statement came through.

However, if the official version is rejected

then the timing of Blanchard's leave takes on a new significance. Several researchers believe that the flying saucer crashed on the night of 4 July and that military men moved in to cordon off the area on the morning of 5 July. If this is true, it means that the USAAF was aware of the crashed saucer the day before Blanchard decided to go on leave.

▲ Lt Col Payne Jennings took over command of Roswell air base when Blanchard went on his controversial leave, soon after the Roswell Incident hit the headlines.

A Real Holiday?

The conclusion that some researchers have reached is that Blanchard's leave was directly related to the flying saucer crash. It is suggested that as soon as the crash was confirmed, Blanchard was put in charge of the operation to collect all the wreckage, keep the public out of the way and ensure a secure and secretive handover of the flying saucer wreckage to higher authorities.

Blanchard's usual routine duties might have got in the way of this assignment, so it is conjectured that he was ordered to go on official leave while he was, in fact, undertaking his new task. Certainly, nobody has been able to come up with any evidence as to where Blanchard went and what he did in those three weeks other than his own explanation.

The dates and evidence certainly fit the idea that Blanchard was, in reality, dealing with the crashed saucer crisis. On the other hand if Blanchard had known on 6 July that he would be leaving his base to undertake the secretive transfer of a crashed saucer, why would he have announced that very same crashed saucer in a press release before going?

The answer might be that this was all part of a carefully prearranged scheme to kill the story and ensure secrecy. The theory certainly fits the facts so far as they can be established, but it must be admitted that there is no direct evidence that the theory is true. It is, however, supported by several researchers so it should be explored.

The theory assumes that an alien spaceship did, indeed, crash outside Roswell and that it did so on the night of 2 or 4 July 1947. The USAAF found the crashed saucer soon after dawn on the day following the crash. At this point, the cover-up began to be organized from the highest levels within the USAAF. Initially, civilians on the site were ushered away and a security cordon thrown around the Crash Site to keep away anyone in the

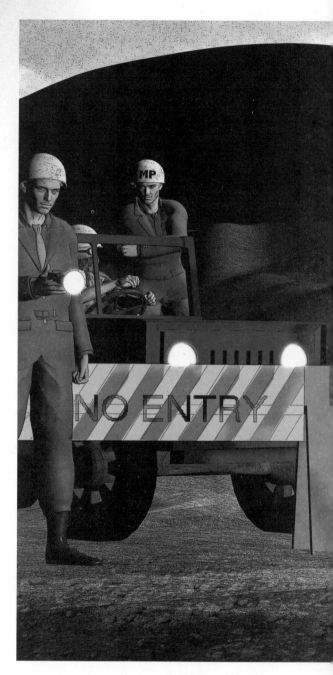

area. At the same time Colonel Blanchard was instructed to apply for 'leave' as a cover for his involvement in the retrieval and clear-up operation. He was told to go as soon as he could without his sudden departure leading to any suspicions. It is assumed that Blanchard thought that it would take him until 8 July to tie up any loose ends, and so applied for leave to begin on that date.

Those organizing the retrieval and cover-up must have hoped that their swift actions on the day the saucer was discovered would be enough. The few civilian witnesses seemed to have been silenced and the military personnel could probably be relied upon to keep quiet. Blanchard could go on his 'leave' to lead

the secretive clear-up process, then 'return to duty' when his task was completed, leaving no paper trail for future investigators to follow.

However, there was always the risk that one of the civilians who had seen the crashed saucer would go to the press. A strategy was needed that would be robust enough to cope with such a circumstance. In the event, it was not a civilian who had seen the Crash Site who went to the press but the rancher Mac Brazel, who had found some wreckage on his land. The word got out via the radio station before the find was officially reported to the USAAF, and consequently, before Brazel could be persuaded to remain silent.

According to this reconstructed chain of events, the press release authorized by Blanchard was already prepared and ready to go as part of the cover-up. All that was required was for Blanchard to insert the name of the witness who had gone to the press and the claims he or she had made. Once aware of Brazel's claims, Blanchard duly inserted the relevant information and then phoned Haut to order him to issue the press release.

Once the story had been given enough time

▲ A military cordon around an area of desert was set up and access strictly controlled.

The press release authorized by Blanchard was already prepared and ready to go as part of the cover-up.

to run around the media of the USA, the press conference in Ramey's office was organized to kill the story. Ramey had, according to this scenario, already prepared the remains of a crashed weather balloon so that it could be paraded in front of the press. Again, all that was needed was for Ramey to precede his press conference with some charade designed to convince the reporters that what they were seeing was part of the wreckage allegedly seen by whichever witness had come forward. Marcel's flight to Fort Worth with material from the Debris Field and its hurried replacement with balloon wreckage performed this role admirably.

The alleged cover-up then saw the Pentagon issue statements designed to denounce the witness and his alleged saucer. This is, indeed, what happened. Mac Brazel was first escorted to the Roswell media to change his story, then kept on the Roswell air base until the USAAF high command could be certain that the story of a crashed saucer had been killed in the media. Anyone who sought to reopen the case would be faced by the seemingly solid story of some wreckage seen by a Roswell civilian, which was later positively identified by the military authorities in front of reporters as being a harmless weather balloon.

Later Testimonies

Once the media had been thrown off the scent and had lost interest in the story, the loose ends in Roswell could continue to be tied up and the truth suppressed. Witnesses to the events that followed were mostly interviewed in the 1980s and 1990s. They were very often certain that the events that they saw took place about the time of the fuss in the press about a crashed saucer, but almost without exception could not recall the precise date of the happenings. Some researchers have sought to assign dates to these events to try to fit them in more closely to the Roswell Incident. While in

some instances there is evidence that the events took place in July, it is not really possible to be more precise than that.

Typical was cowhand Bud Payne who worked on a ranch near Corona. He recalled that at about this time he had been rounding up stray cattle on his land when he went further south than was usual and got close to the pastures of the Foster Ranch. As he chased a steer, Payne was surprised when a military jeep came into sight and a soldier flagged him down. Payne stopped and was informed by the soldier that the lands to the south were temporarily off limits to civilians due to a military exercise of some undefined nature but supreme importance. Payne turned around and rode off north, watched by the soldier until he was out of sight.

Aircrew working for the First Air Transport Unit recalled being summoned at short notice to fly crates out of Roswell amid conditions of great secrecy. It was unusual for crates to be moved under armed guard and to be escorted by senior officers. One of the crates was met at Fort Worth by a military medical officer who, it is thought, specialized in the care of dead bodies. These men included Lieutenant Robert Shirkey, Sergeant Robert Slusher and Robert Smith.

Brigadier General Exon

One key witness to the cover-up has been Brigadier General Arthur E. Exon. In July 1947 Exon was a junior officer who was stationed at Wright Field air base, the secretive base to which the wreckage of the Roswell saucer was allegedly taken. By the 1960s, Exon was commander of the conventional USAAF units at what by then had become Wright-Patterson. Although he was never privy to the exact work of the top secret units on the base, he was involved in supporting them and was in a position to know the comings and goings of the personnel. His own personal courage cannot be doubted. Exon flew 135 combat missions during the Second World War, being shot down over Germany in 1944 and spending more than a year as a prisoner of war. His promotion to brigadier general came in 1965, some years prior to his retirement.

Exon's testimony was collected in the later 1980s and early 1990s. It falls into two distinct sections. There is firstly his evidence about what happened in 1947, most of which is second-hand. Secondly, there are his first-hand accounts of events in the 1960s.

Exon's only piece of first-hand evidence about 1947 relates to a trip he made to Roswell sometime in the autumn of that year, probably in November. During the flight to Roswell, Exon recalls that the man with him – who was from the more secretive sections of Wright Field – pointed out of the window to show him the site where 'that thing we have been studying' came down. Exon recalls seeing an area of scrubland marked by vehicle tracks and cleared vegetation. There was also a gouge in the ground as if something heavy, such as an aircraft, had struck it.

Exon recalls that there were two impact sites, one to the north-west of the other. The more north-westerly site seemed to him to be the larger and more impressive. This is an interesting remark as it was the Debris Field on the Foster Ranch that lay to the north-west of the Crash Site off the highway from Roswell to Vaughn. It may be that, from the air, the Debris Field looked more impressive as it was the more spread out of the two sites.

Exon claimed to recall the weeks after the alleged Roswell saucer crash clearly. He said that some quantities of material were flown into Wright Field at this time for testing and analysis. Exon never claimed to have seen or handled any of this material himself, but to have spoken to the men who did.

According to Exon the material that came to Wright Field was wreckage, not a complete craft. It was all in pieces, most of them quite

small. This debris was subjected to a full range of tests, including chemical analysis, stress tests, compression tests, flexing and microscopic study. These revealed that the material was of several different types. Some of it was incredibly strong, while other pieces could be torn almost as easily as paper. A special project was set up to study the material from Roswell, but it was unable to come to any firm conclusions. 'It had them pretty puzzled,' Exon

▲ Brigadier General Exon saw what was probably the Crash Site from the air in 1947.

remembered. Apparently some of the specialists thought that the debris might have come from Russia, but others were of the opinion that it was so advanced that it could not have come from anything on Earth and was, by implication, of alien manufacture.

Exon also recalled that bodies had been found in the same place as the wreckage. He knew very little about these bodies, other than that they had come to Wright Field for study.

Another witness from Wright Field in 1947 was Sarah Holcomb, a civilian secretary who had high security clearance and who handled the typing and despatch of much highly sensitive documentation. She remembered a number of top secret flights coming in from New Mexico in the summer of 1947, together with rumours that they contained pieces of a crashed flying saucer and the bodies of its crew.

> **Some of the specialists thought that the debris might have come from Russia, but others were of the opinion that it was so advanced that it could not have come from anything on Earth.**

Regarding his later involvement at Wright-Patterson, Exon could be more definite. Again, he was not privy to the secrets of the more confidential areas and staff, but he was responsible for supporting their actions. He was aware of the procedure for collecting and recovering anything of an unusual nature that was to be studied by the teams of scientists investigating foreign – or alien – weapons and technology. First a phone call would come from the Pentagon ordering Exon to provide an aircraft to take an initial investigatory team to the location of the find. The team usually comprised eight to fifteen men. Once a preliminary investigation was complete, a request for a transport aircraft to carry the item found would be made. Exon would arrange for the flight to go out, crewed by men with security clearance, and for the handling of the material when it came back. So far as the evidence is available, this seems to have been a very similar procedure to that followed at Roswell in 1947. While not conclusive, this would seem to indicate that whatever was found at Roswell was thought to be of interest to the teams at Wright Field.

Meanwhile, the USAAF in Roswell was keeping on top of the situation. In the months

after the incident, Mac and Bill Brazel came across a number of scraps of debris that the military had missed in their clean-up of the site. According to Bill's later recollection, this material generally conformed with that found by his father, but with one difference. Bill remembered that he had found some thread-like material. He said that it looked like a fine silk thread, but that it lacked the fibres of silk so that it was more like a wire. It was also astonishingly strong. 'You could take it in two hands and try to snap it, but it wouldn't snap at all.'

CONFISCATION OF DEBRIS

One evening in the summer of 1949, Bill Brazel mentioned the collection of bits and pieces in public. Next day a USAAF captain named Armstrong arrived at Brazel's home with three men. They asked Bill to hand over the material, which he was happy to do being told that it was a matter of national security. Armstrong then asked Bill Brazel to show him the area of land where the material had been found. Again, Bill did as he was asked. As his men began searching the pasture, Captain

▲ The Debris Field as remembered by Bill Brazel. Military personnel have arrived in jeeps and are carefully removing every scrap of wreckage, including lightweight beams and pieces of fabric.

► A piece of the debris as described by Bill Brazel. The debris that he kept was later confiscated by the military.

'The tape was about two or three inches wide and had flower-like designs on it. The 'flowers' were faint, a variety of pastel colors.'

Armstrong asked Bill Brazel to contact him at the Roswell base if he ever found any more debris in the area. Brazel agreed, but never did find any more material.

When asked in the 1980s if what he had found and handled could have come from a weather balloon, Bill Brazel was adamant. 'No, I can answer that for sure. We've picked up balloons and any time we found one we always turned it in because there was a reward for them. This was no balloon.' But by the time he was asked the question, Bill had none of the wreckage left as it had been taken away by Captain Armstrong.

Bill may have been certain, but his younger sister, Bessie, had a different story to tell. Interviewed in 1994 she recalled that the debris seemed nothing out of the ordinary.

The debris looked like pieces of a large balloon which had burst. The pieces were small, the largest I remember measuring about the same as the diameter of a basketball. Most of it was a kind of double-sided material, foil-like on one side and rubber-like on the other. Sticks, like kite sticks, were attached to some of the pieces with a whitish tape. The tape was about two or three inches [5–7 cm] wide and had flower-like designs on it. The 'flowers' were faint, a variety of pastel colors. The foil-rubber material could not be torn like ordinary aluminum foil. I do not recall anything else about the strength or other properties of what we picked up. I remember dad [Mac Brazel] saying 'Oh, it's just a bunch of garbage'.

The Cover-Up

These views of Bessie's are often denounced by those seeking to establish that whatever crashed at Roswell was of alien construction, but they are often strangely ignored by those seeking a more normal explanation as well. Of course, Bessie was only 14 in 1947 and she had grown up in a fairly remote area of the USA. Perhaps investigators felt that an impressionable teenage girl without much first-hand experience of the rapidly developing modern technology of the 1940s was not the most reliable of witnesses. Nevertheless, Bessie was always quite clear that she was remembering events accurately. But then, by the 1980s she did not have any of the debris to show investigators either.

From all the evidence available, it seems certain that the USAAF did organize a cover-up at Roswell in 1947. Whether it was limited to requesting witnesses to remain silent for reasons of national security – or if it was much more widespread and required the false leave of Colonel Blanchard to operate it – is very much an open question. But it was certainly effective.

Only the dissatisfaction of Major Marcel spoiled this seamless cover-up – and even then it took decades before Marcel was taken seriously by anyone. But if there was, in fact, an alien spacecraft crash at Roswell in 1947, and if the USAAF have been covering up the truth for all these years, then the crashed saucer must have spent the past sixty years somewhere. The question is where?

7

Area 51

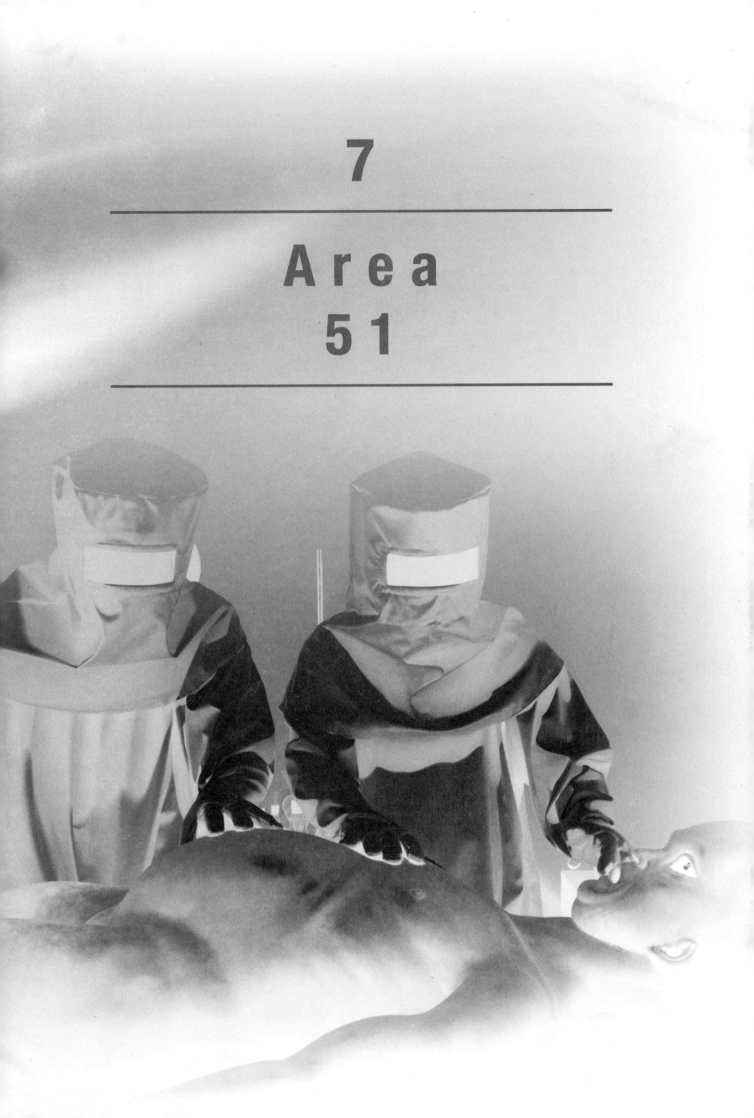

▲ ▶
That Area 51 exists is not in doubt, nor that the military keep civilians out of it, as these signs show, but what goes on there is a closely guarded secret.

ANY RESEARCHERS have concluded that the cover-up perpetrated by the USAAF at Roswell in 1947 was so comprehensive that the chances of discovering any real detail about the object that came down into the scrubland are tiny. Even those who firmly believe that an alien spaceship did crash at Roswell accept that they are unable to deduce much about it from the available evidence.

Most agree that the craft was shaped like the heel of a boot, contained the dead bodies of up to six crew members and was composed of material quite unlike anything then available on Earth, but beyond that not much is known.

Having given up on finding out details from those involved at Roswell, some researchers have decided to widen their investigations. It is unarguable that if an alien spacecraft crashed at Roswell and was retrieved by the USAAF then something must have happened to it next. If the evidence for a crash cannot be definitively established from events at Roswell, they argue, then perhaps it can be established elsewhere.

▲ Area 51 as seen from space. The runways, buildings and roads are clearly visible, though again what happens on the base is kept hidden.

REVERSE ENGINEERING

If the USAAF really did come across a craft of incredibly sophisticated design – as an alien spaceship undoubtedly would be – the most likely thing for them to do with it would be to subject it to reverse engineering. This is a well understood and widely practised technique used by governments and private corporations around the world. It involves handing a

piece of hardware over to specialist scientists and technicians who have expertise in that type of product. They are then asked to work back from the finished product to deduce how it was made – and to suggest ways in which a copy could be produced.

Reverse engineering very often allows commercial companies to understand how their business rivals are manufacturing successful items. It also allows governments to keep track of what actual or potential enemy states are capable of producing for their military. There are instances of successful weapons or pieces of military kit being rapidly copied by enemies using reverse engineering.

One of the more famous examples of military reverse engineering took place at about the time of the Roswell Incident. During the later stages of the Second World War, the USAAF's most successful long-range heavy bomber was the Boeing B-29 'Superfortress'. This massive four-engined bomber could carry up to 9 tons (8.2 tonnes) of bombs to targets 900 miles (1,450 km) distant. It was the aircraft flown by the 509th based at Roswell, and was used extensively in the Korean War. In Korea one of these huge bombers suffered mechanical failure and was forced down virtually intact so that it fell into the hands of the Soviets. The Russians reverse engineered the B-29 as they were in need of a long-range bomber themselves for the developing Cold War.

The resulting aircraft was dubbed the 'Tupolev Tu4' by the Russians and proved to be a highly successful machine. There was, however, a puzzle which the Soviet technicians were never able to solve. When they were examining their captured B-29, they found three small but perfectly round holes near the base of the tail fin. The Soviet engineers subjected the holes to every test that they could think of, but were entirely unable to work out what their purpose was. Convinced that Boeing would not include a

small detail like this without a reason, the Soviets included three identical small holes in their Tu4 bombers. Only much later did they realize that the holes were, in fact, bullet holes picked up by the B-29 over Korea.

The Soviet reverse engineering project on the B-29 had taken several months of combined effort by teams of dozens of scientists and technicians, while the process of producing the Tu4 had taken months more work by hundreds of engineers and factory workers. Any effort by the USAAF to reverse engineer a flying saucer could be expected to absorb equally large numbers of men over protracted periods of time.

In 1947 the most likely place for such an endeavour to be undertaken was the Wright Field air base in Ohio. It was here that the USAAF Foreign Technology Division (FTD) was based. This was the unit tasked with studying captured foreign weaponry and deducing its capabilities. During the then recently ended Second World War, the FTD

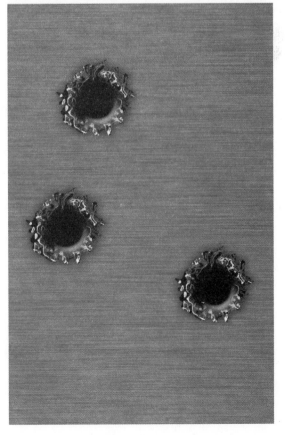

▲ The Russian bomber, the Tupolev Tu4 was a reverse engineered copy of the American B-29. It reputedly included three small holes that were, in fact, bullet holes on the original.

◀ Bullet holes like those found by Soviet technicians on the tail fin of the captured B-29.

had proved itself to be invaluable, especially when studying Japanese military aircraft. It was the FTD which had studied the massively successful Japanese fighter, the Mitsubishi Reisen, better known by its translated name of Zero. The Zero was fast, highly manoeuvrable and packed a punch with an armament of two machine guns and twin 20 mm cannon. However, study of a downed example by the FTD revealed it to have a fragile tail section and to lack self-sealing fuel tanks. These weaknesses were then exploited by US pilots to achieve combat superiority over the Zero by 1943.

THE BLUE ROOM

It has long been rumoured that within the FTD at what is now Wright-Patterson Air Force Base there is an inner section which is subject to the very highest levels of security. Not even those who work on the most sensitive of FTD projects are allowed access to this area, nor are they allowed to know what lies within it. This area is sometimes called Hangar 18 or Building 18, but is often known by the rather more enigmatic and mysterious name of 'The Blue Room'. It is likely that The Blue Room, or something similar, does exist on Wright-Patterson but what it might contain is quite unknown.

Among UFO researchers, it is usually held that The Blue Room contains the saucer that crashed at Roswell in 1947. Some think that it also contains the remains of other crashed UFOs, or bits and pieces of alien spacecraft that have been recovered from time to time.

"At what is now Wright-Patterson Air Force Base there is an inner section which is subject to the very highest levels of security.

Some believe that the bodies of the aliens found at Roswell are also stored here.

Sometime after he stepped down from the Senate, Republican Senator Barry Goldwater revealed that he had taken the stories about The Blue Room very seriously. When he was chairman of the Senate Intelligence Committee in the early 1960s, Goldwater had diligently sought to understand as much as he could about the security and intelligence services of the US military so that he could both lobby on their behalf, and seek to rein them in when necessary. Apparently the only time that he ever received a firm refusal from the military came when he approached the head of the USAAF, General Curtis LeMay, to ask about the FTD. LeMay was happy to answer all of Goldwater's questions, albeit under the promise of absolute secrecy, until The Blue Room was mentioned. LeMay refused point blank to answer any questions about the place. He would not allow Goldwater entry and would not even permit him to talk to any of the personnel who worked there; indeed, LeMay refused even to say who they were. Goldwater came away from the meeting convinced that there was a real Blue Room and that it contained something so explosively secret that only a very few senior military men, and the US President, knew what it was.

If an alien spacecraft was captured in 1947, it would almost certainly have gone to Wright Field. Brigadier General Exon is only the most credible of several witnesses who have come forward to give evidence that something unusual did, in fact, arrive at Wright Field from New Mexico at about this time.

If the crashed saucer was taken to Wright Field for study, the entire project would have been subject to the tightest possible security. It would also have been open to control from the very highest levels within the US military and government. Given the practices of the time, the most likely scenario would have been the establishment of a committee of men drawn from both the military and the government that was answerable to the office of the US President.

PROJECT MAJESTIC TWELVE

In December 1984 sensational new evidence emerged that just such a body had existed and that it had been tasked with dealing with the Roswell Incident. The body was allegedly codenamed Project Majestic Twelve. Among UFO researchers it is generally known as Majestic 12, or more simply MJ12.

The MJ12 affair began in December 1984 when film-maker Jaime Shandera, who had an interest in UFOs, received an undeveloped roll of film in the post. Shandera had the film developed and then called in UFO researcher William Moore, who was also working on the

◀ The Majestic Twelve (MJ12) affair began when film-maker Jaime Shandera received a mysterious packet through the post.

▲ President Harry Truman was in office at the time of the Roswell Incident.

▲ President Dwight Eisenhower is alleged to have received a top-level briefing on the UFO issue, a fact referred to in the MJ12 documents.

Roswell Incident. The film proved to contain photographs of a number of documents that were dated 18 November 1952. The documents claimed to be a highly secret briefing paper on the subject of UFOs prepared for the then President-elect Dwight Eisenhower.

The two-month period of time between when a US President is elected and when he takes office is used by the various branches of government to brief the incoming President on policy items. Most of these are not at all secret, but the briefings are known routinely to include all manner of highly sensitive military and diplomatic secrets with which the President will need to be familiar once in office. The MJ12 documents, at first sight, appeared to be one such briefing paper prepared on the subject of UFOs.

The paper stated that President Harry Truman had set up a panel of top ranking military and government officials, together with a few scientists, to handle the entire UFO phenomenon. Those on this panel – the Majestic Twelve – included the head of the CIA and the Defense Secretary. The group also included USAF General Hoyt Vandenberg who, in 1947, had taken control of the media relations regarding the Roswell Incident. The paper contained the then current appraisal of UFO study by the group to assist Eisenhower in his work as President.

The key claims of the MJ12 documents were that UFOs were definitely alien spacecraft and that several 'saucers' had been either shot down by the USAAF or retrieved after they had crashed. Although Roswell was not mentioned by name, it was quite clear from the circumstances described that one of the saucer crashes described in the MJ12 documents was the 1947 Roswell Incident. More astonishing still was the claim in MJ12 that one of the aliens found at the Roswell Crash Site had been alive when the military arrived. The alien, it was said, had survived for some months before eventually dying of unknown causes.

Shandera and Moore then set about trying to establish whether the MJ12 documents were genuine or fake. Their task was made more difficult by the fact that they did not have the original documents, but only photographs of them. The photos were shown to former CIA personnel and senior government officials, who all agreed that they looked authentic. The documents used the correct typefaces, phraseology and vocabulary for the period from which they were alleged to come. The men listed as being part of MJ12 were all men who had been alive at the time and who had held positions that would have made them sensible choices for inclusion on the panel. The date of 18 November 1952 turned out to be the exact day on which Eisenhower had received a security briefing from the USAF. Without the original documents, of course, it was impossible to prove if they were real or not.

SUSPICIOUS DEATH

The MJ12 documents contained several papers that had been written by or to Truman's first Defense Secretary, James Forrestal. In late March 1948, Forrestal was said to have suffered a mental breakdown – though details are unclear. What is known is that he was taken to a hospital by security staff. One witness remembered Forrestal trying to talk to him about 'people out to get me' and stating 'I won't be allowed to leave here alive', before the security men moved in and hustled him away. During his stay in hospital, Forrestal was allowed to see only his sons, Truman and a couple of men who were named as being part of MJ12. Although he repeatedly asked to see

> ## The official explanation was that Forrestal had committed suicide, but many thought he had been murdered.

his brother Henry, this was not allowed. On 21 May Henry Forrestal finally obtained the right to overrule the security services about his brother's treatment. He booked a suite at his local hospital and made arrangements for Forrestal to be transferred there the following day. That very night Forrestal fell from a 16th-floor window at the hospital.

The official explanation was that Forrestal had committed suicide, but many thought he had been murdered. If the MJ12 documents were correct, the reason for his murder was that he was no longer trusted by those within the security services who had control over the captured saucer.

A surprise confirmation of the MJ12 documents seemed to come in 1985 when an internal USAF memo dating from July 1954 was found in a case of declassified material at the US National Archives. This mentioned in

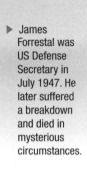

James Forrestal was US Defense Secretary in July 1947. He later suffered a breakdown and died in mysterious circumstances.

passing that a meeting between senior USAF officers and President Eisenhower, which was due to have taken place a few days after the memo was written, should include 'the MJ12 Special Studies Project report'. There was nothing in the memo to indicate what MJ12 was or what the report stated, but it did seem to prove that a body called MJ12 existed.

The MJ12 documents remain deeply controversial. Some researchers point to apparent inconsistencies within them and to dating problems regarding the movements of the people named. They have also pointed out that what purports to be the signature of President Truman is, in fact, a carbon copy of a signature from a known historic document. If the signature is faked, the argument goes, then it is likely that the entire collection of documents are forgeries. Other researchers prefer to believe that the MJ12 documents are genuine. It is likely that we shall never know for certain – unless the originals ever turn up for study.

The MJ12 papers are not the only sources to state that one of the aliens on the crashed saucer at Roswell survived the impact.

TUNGATE'S TESTIMONY

Intriguingly, the MJ12 papers are not the only sources to state that one of the aliens on the crashed saucer at Roswell survived the impact. In the 1990s a new witness came forward in the shape of Richard Tungate. Tungate claimed that in 1952, when he was an officer in the USAF, he had been sent to Roswell to sort through old files. His task was to distinguish between the mass of routine reports and data which were no longer needed and could be thrown out, and the files that were still relevant and needed to be kept. Such sorting of files is normal routine in the military and most government departments.

According to Tungate, his instructions included the order to destroy all papers that referred to a certain woman who had been based at Roswell in 1947. He could not recall the name when interviewed, but it seemed to link to the enigmatic nurse who, according to Glenn Dennis, had left Roswell abruptly in 1947 and had then been killed in an accident in Britain.

While going through the records, Tungate says that he came across some highly secret files that had been mistakenly put away with the routine documents. These referred to a

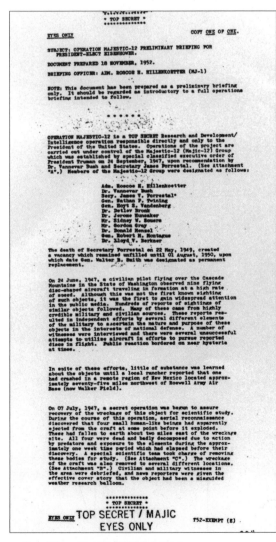

▲ One of the enigmatic MJ12 documents.

crashed alien spacecraft, dead crew members and one survivor. Tungate says that the alien survivor was referred to in the documents as 'EBE', apparently short for 'Extraterrestrial Biological Entity'.

As if this was not enough, Tungate claimed to have later met EBE. He said that having found and read the secret files, he confronted his senior officer on the subject and was then transferred to the unit dealing with it. EBE was short, Tungate claimed, but generally of humanoid shape. Its eyes were large but not of the deep black oval form reported by those who say that they have been abducted by aliens. The being was able to communicate by telepathic means; the only vocalization that

> **The being was able to communicate by telepathic means; the only vocalization that it could make was a harsh rasping noise.**

it could make was a harsh rasping noise. Tungate reported that he thought EBE was unhappy at being kept in confinement and being subjected to various experiments. It wanted to go home. Tungate claimed that he did not know what happened to the alien after their meeting.

Whether or not Tungate can be believed is a topic of disagreement among researchers. His dramatic testimony would, if true, confirm that an alien spaceship did crash at Roswell and that the USAF is still covering up the truth. On the other hand, Tungate was only 21 at the time of his claimed file sifting at Roswell and such duties are usually performed by older officers who can be relied upon to know the difference between a document that is worth keeping and one that can be binned. He has also made some mistakes regarding information in other evidence that he has recounted.

AREA 51

Among Tungate's claims was that the crashed saucer from Roswell had been taken not to Wright Field but to a highly secretive base deep in the Nevada Desert: the notorious 'Area 51'. This military base became famous in the early 1980s when it was revealed that the huge complex was not marked on any maps and, officially at least, did not exist. Since then the history of Area 51 has been fairly well established, though what has gone on there is barely known.

Area 51 was founded in 1954 when 90,000 acres (364 km^2) of government-owned desert about 120 miles (190 km) north of Las Vegas was fenced off and secured against civilian intruders. Inside the fence was built a military airfield together with an extensive CIA base and a factory handed over to the high-tech development arm of the Lockheed Aircraft Corporation. There were other units based there, but their existence is shadowy and their role uncertain. The main purpose of Area 51 was to enable the development and production of secret military and CIA hardware.

By its very nature this work was highly secretive but some of what took place there has come to light. In the mid-1950s, for instance, Area 51 was the site where the U-2 spy plane was designed, tested and built. This remarkable aircraft was able to fly at altitudes of over 70,000 ft (21,000 m) at high speed and over long distances. It was designed to fly over the Soviet Union and China to take photos of military bases and other places of interest to the CIA and the American military. Such flights were, of course, totally illegal, so the U-2 was designed to fly so high and so fast that it could not be brought down by Soviet fighters or missiles. The US government denied Soviet claims that it was sending spy aircraft over their territory, but was forced to admit the truth in May 1960 when pilot Francis Gary Powers was shot down over Soviet land. Although most of the

Area 51

▲ The U-2 spy plane was developed at Area 51 in the 1950s but its existence was not admitted until many years later.

◀ The SR-71 spy plane was designed to replace the U-2 and was tested at Area 51.

▲ The B2 Spirit Stealth Bomber was tested at Area 51 and is now known to have been mistaken for a UFO on several occasions in the 1980s.

spying activity once undertaken by U-2 aircraft is now performed by satellites, the U-2 remains in front line service.

Another aircraft developed at Area 51 was the SR-71 Blackbird, a spy plane again produced by Lockheed for the CIA. The Blackbird entered service in 1964 and, unlike the U-2, none have ever been lost to enemy action. This aircraft was designed to fly at 80,000 ft (24,000 m) and to reach a speed of Mach 3. At such speed, the metal skin of the aircraft heats up to over 400 degrees, causing

it to expand. As a result the planes were fitted with panels that had gaps between them when the aircraft rested on the ground, only joining together once it got into the air. The Blackbird was retired from service in 1998 due to increasing costs.

More recently, the B2 Stealth Bomber and F117 Stealth Fighter have both been produced at Area 51. These futuristic, black, angular aircraft first entered service in 1980, but did not come to public notice until they carried out highly successful bombing missions during

▶ The F117 Nighthawk Stealth Fighter with its anti-radar capabilities was tested at Area 51 before entering service with the USAF.

the 1990 Gulf War, fought to liberate Kuwait from Iraqi occupation. The ability of the stealth aircraft to fly undetected by radar ensured that they were able to penetrate deep within enemy airspace with impunity.

Meanwhile, in 1980, the US government had publicly admitted that Area 51 did exist, but remained secretive about what went on there. As soon as the base was identified it became a focus for aviation enthusiasts who flocked there in the hope of spotting some secret and as yet unacknowledged aircraft. In response to this the USAF acquired a further 4,000 acres (16 km^2) of desert, which effectively deprived civilian visitors – and foreign spies – of any vantage point overlooking the base.

The tight security that has always surrounded Area 51 has excited interest. In the 1980s it was admitted that within Area 51 there was an even more secretive section known only as 'S-4'. As with The Blue Room at Wright-Patterson air base, S-4 has been the subject of UFO-related rumours. The most persistent of these is that the saucer that crashed at Roswell is housed in S-4 and that it is here that reverse engineering has been taking place. Indeed, it is widely alleged among UFO researchers that the highly advanced flight technology undoubtedly being developed at Area 51 is largely based on reverse engineering of the saucer.

In 1989 the veil of secrecy around Area 51 seemed to be shattered when a scientist named Robert Lazar went public with claims that he had worked in S-4 and had become privy to the most astonishing government and military secrets.

ASSASSINATION FEAR

At first Lazar spoke only to researchers and only under conditions of secrecy. But in March 1989 he went public when he took part in a documentary on local Nevada television.

Lazar said that the reason he had decided to go public was because he feared that the CIA was planning to assassinate him to ensure his silence. By telling everything that he knew openly and in public, Lazar hoped to remove any motive that the security services might have for killing him. As a result he poured out a story of great detail and complexity.

According to this tale, Lazar had been working as an electronics engineer in California when he was approached by men claiming to be from US Navy intelligence in December 1987. The men offered him a job of the utmost national importance and secrecy. Lazar said that he agreed. As a first step he, along with other California-based scientists, was picked up in a bus with blacked-out windows and driven for hours. Eventually the bus arrived at a military establishment in a

> Once there he was subjected to a number of tests that included drinking a glass of a mysterious viscous yellow fluid and being hypnotized.

desert area; Lazar would later learn that he was in Area 51. Once there he was subjected to a number of tests that included drinking a glass of a mysterious viscous yellow fluid and being hypnotized. Having apparently passed these tests, Lazar says that he was hired.

His employment at Area 51 allegedly lasted until March 1989. Lazar would be picked up in the blacked-out bus and driven there, and he would stay for several days. He would then be driven home for a couple of days' break before again being collected and taken out to the Nevada desert. Lazar claims that he was given a piece of sophisticated technical equipment that he was told was linked to gravitational field manipulation. His task was to reverse engineer it.

there was a zone of stability for a few elements between atomic weights 113 and 118. He has since been proved to be correct by theoretical physicists, which does at least raise an interesting question about where he got his information.

Lazar says that his work on the gravitational device was so successful that he was moved on to more complex projects. Finally he was informed of the origin of these sophisticated devices. They had come from half a dozen or so UFOs that had crashed on Earth and were being stored inside the S-4 facility.

THE 'SPORTS MODEL'

The most complete of these was a sleek, small black UFO about 35 ft (11 m) in diameter. Lazar said this was nicknamed 'the Sports Model' by those working on it. Lazar was, he says, allowed on board the Sports Model once. He found that it was divided into three levels, each with ceilings so low that it was clear that whoever, or whatever, used the craft were significantly shorter than humans. The gravitational devices, which apparently powered the craft, were on the lower level. The central level was occupied by what looked like control consoles and seating. Lazar was never allowed on to the top level. He did witness a test flight of the Sports Model, when it rose gently into the air to hover a few feet above the ground while emitting a pale blue glow from its underside.

Although this craft does not match descriptions given by witnesses to the Roswell crash, one of the others that Lazar claims to have seen, but not examined, is a close match for the descriptions of the Roswell witnesses. Some take this as corroborative evidence of the crash.

It is the latter claim by Lazar that test flights take place that has been seized upon by those UFO enthusiasts who visit the desert around

▲ Robert Lazar has claimed that he worked at Area 51 on a project to reverse engineer a gravitational device recovered from the Roswell saucer.

According to Lazar, the equipment's success relied upon 'element 115'. This material is known in theory, but does not exist on Earth. It is a transuranic superheavy metal with an atomic weight of 115, hence its name. According to conventional science at the time that Lazar first made his claims, such superheavy metals should be unstable and highly radioactive. They would be dangerous to handle and impossible to maintain for long enough to be used for anything practical. When confronted with this, Lazar said that

Area 51. They hope that one day they will catch sight of a UFO being tested by a human pilot. The USAF are, of course, adamant that no UFOs are kept at Area 51 and that the aircraft being seen and tracked on amateur radar are merely test models of research projects of entirely terrestrial origin. Since the USAF will not discuss these projects for military security reasons, however, not everyone is convinced.

According to Lazar, his employment at S-4 ended after he contacted a UFO researcher named John Lear. Lazar took Lear and a small number of others to the Nevada desert to watch what he claimed was going to be a scheduled test flight of the Sports Model. However, a security patrol found them in a restricted area and arrested them. The group were held in custody for a short time and then released. Lazar was held rather longer, and later claimed that he had been threatened with death if he ever revealed what he knew. It was this, he said, that prompted his decision to speak out.

Lazar's claims have been taken seriously by many researchers, and subjected to critical examination by others. The first suspicions were raised by his description of how he was recruited to the security services. Although the details are of necessity kept secret, the general outline of how the security services go about employing staff is well known. These procedures involve stringent background checks, contact with previous employers and friends, in-depth interviews and above all a commitment to employing people with the correct qualifications. None of these seems to have occurred in the recruitment of Lazar. There have also been some concerns over Lazar's past employment history in Nevada, which has not been entirely above board. On the other hand, such facts as can be checked out have proved to be true. Whether his more sensational claims – which cannot be independently checked – are also true cannot be confirmed.

COLONEL CORSO'S STORY

It is not only Lazar who claims to have been involved with reverse engineering projects. Significantly more impressive as a witness has been Colonel Philip Corso, who entered the world of UFO research in 1997. Corso had served on President Eisenhower's National Security Council and reached the rank of colonel, which at once gave what he said a lot of credibility. Of even more relevance to the Roswell story was the fact that in the 1960s he served as the chief of the US Army's Foreign Technology Desk (FTD) at the Pentagon's Research and Development Department.

According to Corso the US government has been using crashed UFOs as the basis for

> **Visiting enthusiasts hope that one day they will catch sight of a UFO being tested by a human pilot.**

reverse engineering projects for more than half a century. Corso says that he knew nothing about this until he took up his post at the FTD, when it was revealed to him the true origin of technical devices that he, and everyone else working on them, had previously been assured came from other Earth countries. Corso said that by far the most productive UFO for reverse engineering had been that which crashed at Roswell in 1947, because it was the most complete of the assorted crashed craft. Corso does not claim to have been at Roswell, so his evidence can add nothing to what is already known about events in July 1947, but he does add a lot of detail about what the US military has done with the craft that have crashed since then.

Corso says that the wreckage and bodies of the aliens were taken first to Wright Field air

▲ Retired USAF
officer Colonel
Philip Corso
being interviewed
at the Crash Site.
Corso claims
to have seen
documents and
supervised
projects that
show the military
was reverse
engineering alien
artefacts and
technology.

base. There the craft was gradually disman-
tled by scientists intent on finding out how it
worked. The various components were sent to
companies such as IBM, Bell Labs and
Hughes Aircraft to be studied and reverse
engineered. The components were released to
private research companies with cover stories
about their capture from Soviet or Chinese
aircraft. The scientists working on them did
not always manage to crack their secrets, so
some devices have remained mysteries.

Other components and devices did yield up
their secrets over the years, according to Corso.
One of the first of these was, Corso claimed, a
night viewing device. This had proved to be a
success because the alien technology for
thermal imaging was not so very different
from that already being developed on Earth.
The success with that project had given the
core team of scientists valuable insight into
how the alien technology worked and allowed
for more dramatic breakthroughs.

the Roswell saucer was lasers. The aliens, according to Corso, had used the laser as a communications device with an almost unlimited range in deep space. They also used lasers as navigational instruments, bouncing beams off distant objects to allow for triangulation readings to be taken. Fibre optic technology was also, said Corso, based on the Roswell saucer, and so were the anti-missile devices of President Reagan's Star Wars initiative.

There could be no doubting Corso's military background and postings. However, his claims were subject to a great deal of criticism. His accounts of the development of several pieces of technical equipment did not match the known facts about private sector research and development. Corso's claims also included some mistakes about military hardware and deployments that should not have been made by an officer in his position.

EMBELLISHED CLAIMS?

Opinion is currently divided among researchers. Some believe that Corso is basically telling the truth as he experienced it. Any mistakes

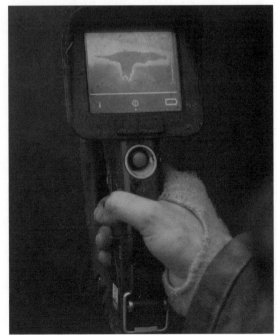

◄ A thermal imaging camera, one of the pieces of technology that Corso claims was obtained from alien sources.

Perhaps the most impressive and important device that Corso claimed was based on alien technology was the integrated circuit chip, which lies at the heart of all modern computers. Corso ascribed the sudden burst of technological development that saw bulky, expensive and unreliable vacuum valves replaced first by transistors and then by integrated circuit boards directly to objects taken from the Roswell saucer.

Another technology credited by Corso to

have been put down to the fact that he was not allowed to copy or retain any of the secret documents that he handled and so was relying on his memory of events and data. Other researchers believe that Corso made his claims as an attempt to make money, and indeed a book that he wrote has sold very well. It is thought that he has taken genuine projects run by the US government but added allegations of alien technology origins to what were, in fact, devices developed on Earth.

One part of Corso's story was immediately tied in to what appears now to have been a carefully constructed hoax, but at the time was thought to be possible final proof of the Roswell UFO crash. Corso said that he read a report that detailed an autopsy carried out on one of the aliens that had died in the crashed saucer at Roswell. Corso gave a lot of detail that he remembered from this report. He said that the bones were fibrous in structure, not cellular like most bones of terrestrial creatures. The lungs and heart showed signs of having been bioengineered, presumably so that they could withstand the rigours of interstellar travel. The musculature indicated that the being came from a planet with a lower gravitational pull than Earth, so it was thought that it would have had difficulty moving in our world.

According to Corso the report said that two of the aliens had survived the crash. One had tried to flee the scene and had been shot by a military guard. The second had been injured in the crash and died a few months later. One doctor suspected that Earth's atmosphere, while not actually toxic to the aliens, did not fully agree with their physiology.

This reference to an autopsy was quickly linked to what was claimed to be a few minutes of movie footage that showed the autopsy taking place. The reports began circulating even before Corso's book hit the shops. According to Ray Santilli, a British film producer, he had been approached by a retired cameraman who had worked for the US military in the 1940s and 1950s. This cameraman claimed to have kept some footage of top secret projects on which he had worked, and now he wanted to sell them. He said he wanted to buy a wedding present for his granddaughter.

Santilli said that at first he was doubtful if the footage would have any great commercial value given that projects classified as highly secret in 1950 would probably be declassified

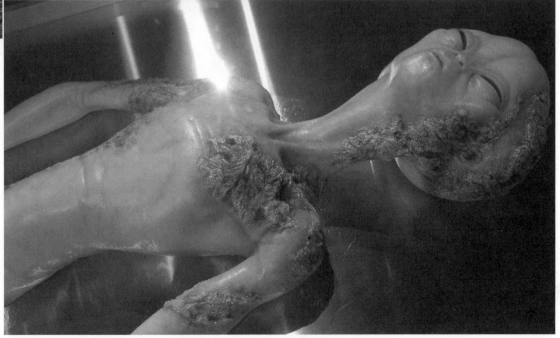

◀ A model of a dead alien with burns and other injuries, like those that are said to have been suffered by the crew of the Roswell saucer.

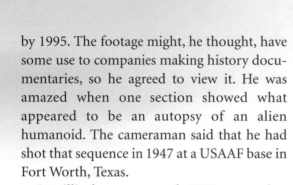

by 1995. The footage might, he thought, have some use to companies making history documentaries, so he agreed to view it. He was amazed when one section showed what appeared to be an autopsy of an alien humanoid. The cameraman said that he had shot that sequence in 1947 at a USAAF base in Fort Worth, Texas.

Santilli then contacted UFO researcher Stanton Friedman, who became interested as he knew that the Roswell debris was reported to have been flown from Roswell air base to the base at Fort Worth. Although none of the witnesses at Roswell had specified that the alien

> **The unanimous verdict was that the footage could have been faked quite easily given access to a moderately well-equipped special effects studio.**

corpses had also gone to Fort Worth, this would make sense. Santilli first showed the film to a private meeting of invited UFO researchers and journalists with an interest in the subject in May 1995. The film was impressive and nothing in it seemed to show anything other than the autopsy of a humanoid body shot in the late 1940s or early 1950s.

HOAX FOOTAGE

It was not long, however, before Santilli's inability to answer questions about the footage began to raise suspicions. The real name of the cameraman who had supplied the footage was not given on the grounds that he wanted to remain anonymous. However, this made it impossible to check the man's service record to see if he had worked for the USAAF in 1947. Nor would Santilli supply a section of the original film so that it could be analyzed to ascertain the date when it had been manufactured.

Sceptics contacted movie special effects experts to ask them if the film could have been faked. The unanimous verdict was that the footage could have been faked quite easily given access to a moderately well-equipped special effects studio. The cost was variously estimated at between $40,000 and $100,000. This would have made producing the 'Alien Autopsy Footage', as it became known, an expensive undertaking. However, if the footage was to be accepted as genuine it could be guaranteed to generate considerable income from selling it to documentary makers, showing it on TV and selling stills to

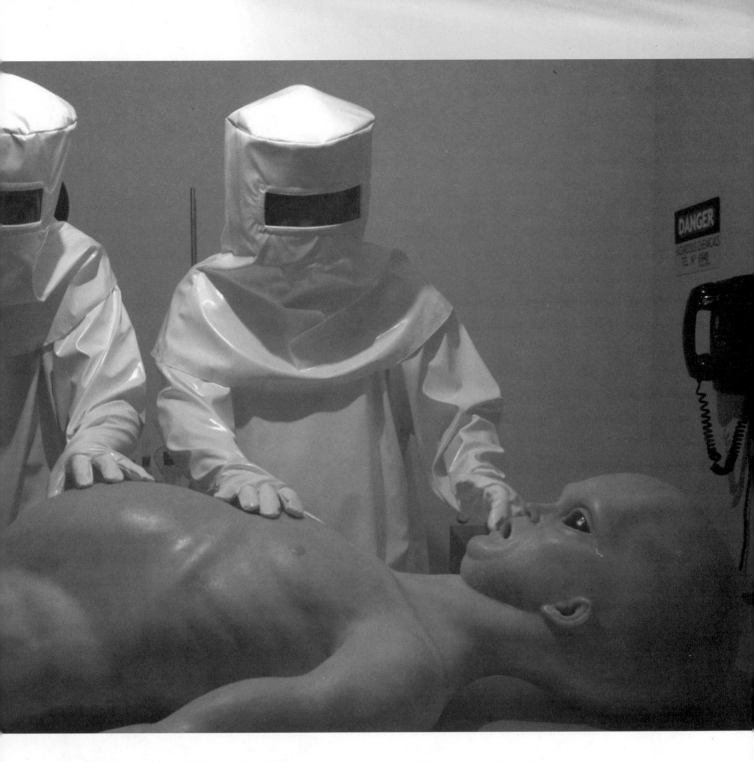

magazine and book publishers. If the footage was a fraud, it was one that had the potential to gain or lose the perpetrator a lot of money.

In the years that followed, doubts about the authenticity of the film began to gain momentum. This culminated in 2006 when the British comedy duo Anthony McPartlin and Declan Donnelly (better known as Ant and Dec) made their own movie. This comic film purported to show the true story behind the Alien Autopsy Footage. It showed the building of a fake mortuary, the construction of a fake alien body and the filming of the hoax. As the movie headed towards cinema release, Santilli went public with an admission that the footage was a fraud.

Santilli claimed that the film was shot in the living room of a rented property in London. John Humphreys, a sculptor, was named as the man who created the dummy alien bodies while the entrails and other pieces of body seen in the film were identified as offal bought from London's famous Smithfield meat market. Humphreys and Santilli had played the roles of the scientists carrying out the autopsy. However, in making this admission, Santilli insisted that the faked footage had actually been a recreation of the genuine film

▲ A scene from the movie *Alien Autopsy* that starred British comic duo Anthony McPartlin and Declan Donnelly (Ant and Dec).

supplied to him. The anonymous cameraman, however, had subsequently demanded it back and refused to show it again.

In 2008 a new alien autopsy film appeared that claimed to be the original. The provenance of this movie is hotly debated, though most researchers think it to be another hoax. It can be seen on YouTube. Another movie on YouTube purports to be an alien autopsy filched from the files of the KGB.

"The Roswell Incident was but one part of this brutal conflict which saw up to nine saucers shot down.

JOHN LEAR'S THEORY

Such apparent fakes and frauds aside, the researchers who had been investigating Area 51, section S-4 and their alleged links to aliens continued to investigate connections between modern technology and the alleged Roswell saucer crash. Among these researchers was John Lear. Lear had developed a theory that accounts not only for the Roswell Incident, but also for numerous other UFO reports and for the allegations of alien abductions. According to this theory, the initial burst of UFO activity in 1947 rapidly led to an undeclared and highly secretive war waged between the USAAF and other Earth air forces on the one side and the alien spacecraft on the other. The Roswell Incident was but one part of this brutal conflict which saw up to nine saucers shot down or forced down by electronic means, and dozens of military aircraft destroyed. It should be remembered that the very first 'flying saucer' report to make the newspapers was made by businessman Kenneth Arnold when he was searching for a military transport aircraft that had crashed in the Cascade Mountains area for unexplained reasons.

This initial phase of armed conflict, Lear claimed, had come to an end in 1950 when the aliens agreed a peace treaty with US President Truman. The terms of this treaty apparently involved the aliens offering their technology to the US government. The secretive S-4 facility at Area 51, it was said, did not contain the crashed remains from Roswell, but was actually staffed by aliens who concentrated on finding a way to interface their technology with that of Earth. In return, the US government agreed to allow the aliens to abduct and conduct experiments upon an agreed number of humans. It is these abduc-

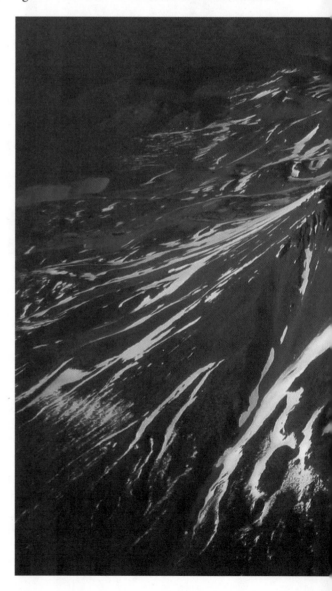

tions that people have been reporting over the past few decades.

Others have since taken up Lear's ideas, expanding or refining them in the light of new evidence – albeit sometimes evidence of a somewhat dubious kind. It has been suggested that S-4 is not the only alien base on Earth. Mount Shasta in California is said to hide a base buried more than a kilometre underground that is run by a race of aliens that are well disposed towards humanity. Very different is the base said to lie near the town of Dulce in New Mexico. This is an advance base for the Greys who, it is said, are bent on

an invasion of Earth and the downfall of mankind. Another race, apparently based in Canada, are said to be the Deros. These violent and vicious beings are interested only in mindless destruction. The sworn enemies of the Deros are said to be the Teros, who are friendly towards mankind.

Several of the different theories agree that the aliens broke the treaty some time in the 1970s by abducting and experimenting upon far more humans than the pact had allowed. While the agreement is thought to have stipulated that the humans subjected to experiments should be allowed to go free gen-

▼ Mount Shasta is said by some to be the site for an underground alien base, hidden a thousand metres beneath the surface.

▲ The many reports of alien abduction in the 1980s and 1990s convinced many researchers that something deeply disturbing was happening.

erally unharmed, the new wave of abductions saw humans killed and mutilated. It was this, rather than any fear of Soviet missiles, which is said to have led President Ronald Reagan to embark on his massively costly and highly controversial 'Star Wars' programme of building armed satellites.

Others believe that the co-operation between the aliens and US government has continued and progressed to become what is called the 'Alternative 3'.

This theory states that Earth will soon become uninhabitable due to climate change and pollution. The elites among governments have realized that the Earth is doomed and want to escape. They have therefore co-operated with the aliens and their abduction experiments in order to gain access to a vast base on Mars where they will be able to survive the impending disaster.

Such theories are viewed by many within the UFO-investigating community as being far-fetched to the point of verging on science fiction. They have all, however, grown out of the idea that UFOs are alien spaceships, and the Roswell Incident has been one of the most important factors in popularizing that idea.

The USAF and US government, of course, have vigorously denied not only the more extreme theories but also the whole notion that unexplained objects in the sky might be alien spacecraft. In particular they have always denied that anything odd at all happened at Roswell in July 1947.

Simple denials have proved not to be enough, so the USAF has put forward its own version of events.

Whether or not that version can be believed must lie at the heart of any attempt to solve the Roswell mystery.

8

The Airforce
Strikes Back

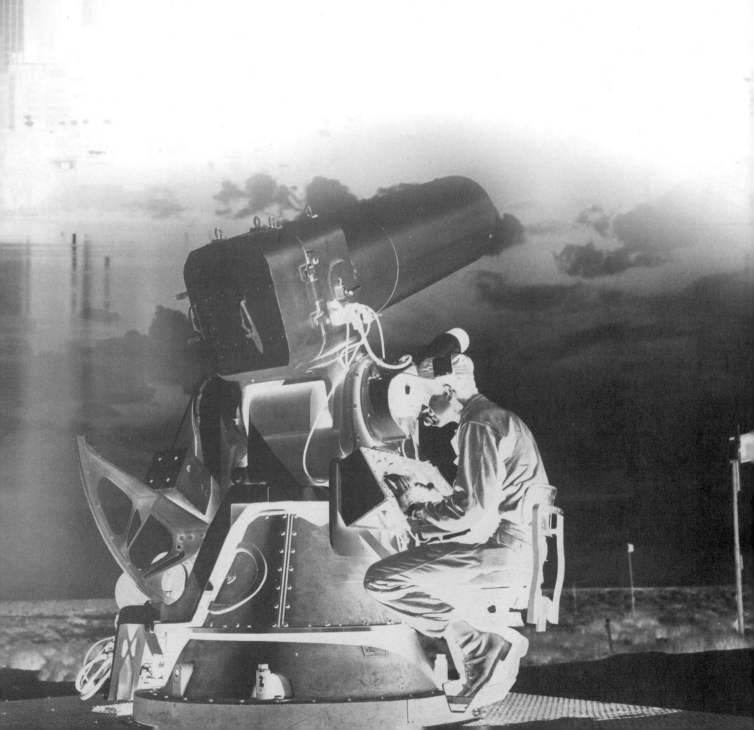

▲ A selection of photographs from the early 20th century showing meteorologists launching balloons to study the weather.

N JULY 1947 THE OFFICIAL explanation issued by the then USAAF for the events in and around Roswell were that rancher Mac Brazel had found some wreckage on his land. Brazel had alerted the authorities who sent the military, in the form of Major Jesse Marcel, to inspect the finds. Marcel had thought that the debris might belong to a flying saucer and had alerted his immediate superior, Colonel Blanchard, to this fact. Blanchard had viewed some of the debris and came to the same conclusion. He had then issued a press release announcing this fact before packing Marcel

and the wreckage off to 8th US Air Force HQ in Fort Worth. Once the wreckage arrived there it was immediately identified as being from a weather balloon. A correction to the original press release was then issued.

At the time this version of events had been widely believed. Indeed, the media of the entire USA had accepted the USAAF statements in their entirety. Most newspapers and radio stations dropped the story at once, and those who continued to cover it carried the weather balloon story uncritically. But if any journalist had taken the trouble to investigate further they would soon have found clues

were not as the USAAF claimed they were.

Mac Brazel had talked to the *Roswell Daily Record* the day after General Ramey issued his weather balloon explanation. In the course of that interview, Brazel stated clearly that he had found two weather balloons on his land before. He then added: 'I am sure what I found was not any weather observation balloon.' It is most unfortunate that Brazel did not elaborate on what the differences were between what he brought in to show Sheriff Wilcox and the weather balloons he had found previously. Given that the media were rapidly losing interest in the story,

nobody asked him. Clearly, however, whatever he had found had struck him as being very odd and unusual. It was unfamiliar enough to cause him to take pieces of it to show to the sheriff.

WEATHER BALLOONS

It is worth bearing in mind the way in which weather balloons were used at this time. First, there was no such thing as a standard weather balloon. They came in various sizes and shapes depending on their purpose. The simplest and most basic weather balloon was designed to carry aloft a lightweight aluminium plate that would reflect a clear radar signal. As the balloon rose it would be moved by the winds. By tracking the aluminium plate on radar, a ground station could discover the speed and direction of winds at different altitudes. Most of these balloons were made of rubber.

Larger balloons were used to carry aloft more complex cargoes that monitored temperature, humidity and other data. These more complex payloads could weigh many pounds and needed much more lifting power to take off and keep airborne. Instead of rubber balloons, it was by the later 1940s becoming usual to use polyethylene balloons. These could be massive affairs, reaching over 200 ft (60 m) in diameter when fully inflated.

All these balloons, of course, had to come down to earth somewhere. Usually, they were tracked on radar so that the teams that had launched them would know roughly where to go to find their instruments and collect their

> To encourage the public to report downed balloons and to maintain good relations, the USAAF offered a reward of $25 for each balloon reported to them.

data. To encourage the public to report downed balloons and to maintain good relations, the USAAF offered a reward of $25 for each balloon reported to them. The payload, whatever it might be, almost always carried a small metal plate giving the phone number that the finder should call to claim the reward.

By his own statement, Brazel had found such balloons before. And yet he believed that the objects he found in July 1947 were something quite different.

It was not only a rancher who thought that there was something odd about the debris. Major Marcel also thought that the detritus had not come from a standard weather balloon. The detailed descriptions of the

> **By the early 1990s … researchers had gathered enough evidence to make the weather balloon explanation for the Debris Field untenable.**

material that he gave were not made until many years later, but by reporting the find to his commanding officer Marcel was making it very clear that he thought he had found something unusual. Neither at the time nor since did Colonel Blanchard make a detailed description of the debris shown to him. Again, however, his action in sending it on to higher authorities for study makes it equally clear that he believed it to be something worth investigating further.

It is credible that a rancher more accustomed to punching cattle and herding sheep might mistake a weather balloon for something unusual. That a reasonably senior officer in military intelligence might make the same mistake is much less likely. Still less credible is the suggestion that a highly experienced colonel commanding the world's most important bomber base would be unable to

recognize a weather balloon. And yet all these things were said by the USAAF at the time to have taken place.

BALLOON SCEPTICS

As the years passed and nobody in the media resurrected the story, the USAF had no need to revise their explanation of events. So when UFO researchers began to investigate the story in the 1980s, the response from the USAF was simply to look back at the files and repeat the original story that the debris found at the Foster Ranch by Mac Brazel was the remains of a perfectly normal weather balloon.

By the early 1990s, however, the Roswell story was becoming so important that the USAF could no longer effectively ignore it. Researchers had gathered enough evidence to make the weather balloon explanation for the Debris Field untenable. There were also a growing number of reports about humanoid bodies being found in the desert and others detailing a crashed flying craft. Still the USAF seemed to view the incident as an annoyance. So far as they were concerned UFOs were not alien spacecraft and it therefore followed that one could not have crashed at Roswell in 1947.

It was this attitude that led the USAF to dismiss any inquiries that it received. When New Mexico's Congressman Steven Schiff began asking questions, he was likewise fobbed off with evasive replies. It is not so easy to evade a congressman as to ignore a private UFO researcher, and Schiff took the matter up with the General Accounting Office (GAO). The GAO in turn asked the USAF to go back over its files and seek to discover what had actually happened in Roswell in July 1947.

Before looking at the evidence unearthed by the exhaustive – and expensive – USAF inquiry, it is important to understand the key theory put forward by the investigators on which they based all their findings. This is that human memory is a frail thing that can

easily make mistakes. Undoubtedly this is true. Looking back over a period of thirty or forty years, as most witnesses to the Roswell Incident were, it is surprisingly easy to misremember things.

Among the more common memory errors that the USAF researchers took into account is the difficulty over recalling dates. People link events to each other rather than to actual dates. A person might remember, for instance, that an event happened just after Christmas, but not be able to remember the year. Another common error is to 'concertina' two similar but different events so that they are recalled as if they were one single event. Thus a person might 'remember' getting a book and a jacket from their wife one Christmas, when in fact the presents were given at different Christmases.

In general, the USAF report puts much more faith in documents that were written at the time than on witness statements made decades later. There can be no doubt that this is a correct attitude, but the two problems that then arise are how much of a person's memory should be discounted and whether or not the contemporary documents were accurate when they were written.

One important conclusion reached by the USAF investigation was that they were dealing essentially with two distinct events. First there was what happened at what has become known as the Debris Field. This was where the wreckage was discovered by Mac Brazel on his ranch, reported to Sheriff George Wilcox, collected by Major Jesse Marcel and dismissed by General Roger Ramey as a weather balloon. This incident

▲ Witnesses have reported seeing stiff, dead alien bodies lying in the desert, but the USAF has put forward what it claims to be a perfectly normal explanation for the reported sightings.

could be tracked clearly in contemporary documents and in the witness statements collected decades after the event. The USAF researchers also found details of this event in the USAF files that they studied.

The second event occurred at the Crash Site, where a downed flying craft and scattered humanoid bodies were reported. This incident was not mentioned in any of the contemporary newspaper or press agency reports but relied exclusively on later eyewitness testimony. The USAF researchers failed to find any trace of this event in the military files that they studied. They came to the conclusion that while the witnesses may have

> **One important conclusion reached by the USAF investigation was that they were dealing essentially with two distinct events.**

been essentially accurate when describing what they saw, they had misremembered the date of the event. The USAF researchers believed that the witnesses had linked the crashed craft to the Debris Field story long after the event – a classic case of 'concertina' memory. They had then set about trying to find an explanation for the reports of a crashed craft and humanoid bodies that would match the statements, but which did not necessarily take place in July 1947.

Many UFO researchers have criticized this decision by the USAF report to separate the Debris Field from the Crash Site so that they form two entirely different events. However, it must be admitted that the witnesses to the Crash Site are not themselves very clear about time. Barney Barnett stated only that it had been before around 1952. Edwin Easley said he had been sent to guard a crash site in the summer, probably of 1947. Those who could be more specific about the time of the crash,

such as William Woody, did not claim to have seen bodies. Witnesses who claimed to have seen a crashed craft and corpses definitely in July 1947 have since mostly been found either to have deliberately lied or to have made serious errors in other parts of their recollections.

This is not to say that the USAF was correct to separate the two events. But it is important to bear in mind that this is what they did and to understand why they did so.

USAF REPORT

Almost the first thing that the USAF report revealed was that whatever had come down on the Foster Ranch and was discovered by Mac Brazel was not a weather balloon. Brazel, Blanchard and Marcel had all been correct in 1947 when they identified what they had found as something new and unusual. There had been no weather balloon launches at the time in which the balloon was not recovered at a known location. In short, there were no lost balloons that could have fallen on the Foster Ranch.

What was recorded in the USAF files, however, was something rather different. Holloman air base lay just outside Alamogordo, some 130 miles (210 km) southwest of Roswell and 100 miles (160 km) south of the Foster Ranch. Stationed there was a highly classified research project that in 1947 was considered both very secret and of immense importance to the security of the USA. This was codenamed Project Mogul. The Mogul project was an attempt by the US military to discover whether the Soviet Union had succeeded in developing an atomic bomb.

The US military had known that their own work on an atomic explosive during the early 1940s would very likely become a target for spies from other countries that wanted their own such weapon. US President Truman had become aware of this as early as June 1945

An atom bomb of the type being carried by the bombers based at Roswell air base in 1947. The secrecy and security surrounding these weapons was both elaborate and strict.

▲ Julius and Ethel Rosenberg after their arrest.

▶ British leader Clement Atlee (left), US President Harry Truman (centre) and Soviet dictator Josef Stalin (right) at the Potsdam Conference.

when he told the Soviet leader Josef Stalin that the USA was developing an atomic bomb. Stalin made it clear that he already knew that such a weapon was under development but professed ignorance at how the project was progressing. In fact, the US research project had already been deeply penetrated by spies working for the Soviet Union.

Electrical engineer Julius Rosenberg had long been a member of the Communist Party before he was recruited in 1942 to work for the KGB. In his turn he recruited a number of other agents, including David Greenglass, who was working on the atomic bomb project at Los Alamos. Among the many thousands of classified military and government documents that Rosenberg sent to the Soviets were key plans of the atomic bomb, supplied by Greenglass. It was not until 1950 that Rosenberg was unmasked as a spy, at which point Greenglass decided to confess everything and give evidence in order to save his own life. Rosenberg and his wife Ethel were executed; Greenglass got 15 years in prison.

In 1947 the Americans were still unaware of the Rosenberg spy ring, but they did know that the Soviets were developing a nuclear weapon. If the Soviets had tested such a weapon it would have produced shock waves in the upper atmosphere, radiation signals and other signs that could – in theory at least – have been detected over the USA at high altitude. Project Mogul was an attempt to get the necessary scientific instrumentation to an altitude high enough to be able to detect such a Soviet atomic test.

The USAF report highlighted the interview with Mac Brazel carried by the *Roswell Daily Record* on 9 July 1947. This article stated:

Brazel related that on June 14 he and an 8-year-old son, Vernon, were about 7 or 8 miles [11–12 km] from the ranch house when they came upon a large area of bright wreckage made up of rubber strips, tinfoil, a rather tough paper and sticks. At the time Brazel was in a hurry to get his round made and he did not pay much attention to it. But he did remark about what he had seen and on July 4 he, his wife, Vernon and a daughter Betty age 14, went back to the spot and gathered up quite a bit of the debris.

This article seemed to put the crash on or before 14 June. If the debris had come from a balloon, the description of the wreckage as 'bright' seemed to indicate that it had come

down within the past fortnight or so. After a period of time longer than that, the rubber and aluminium becomes degraded in the desert sun. Similarly, the description of the rubber as being in 'strips' indicated that it had been blowing about in the wind for several days before it was first seen. This would have given the balloon time to be torn into pieces by being blown around scrubs and thorn bushes. This gives a range of dates of about 1 to 10 June for a balloon to have come down and get into the condition that it was when Brazel first saw it.

According to the new USAF theory, the wreckage found by Brazel was of this new and top secret Mogul balloon launch.

Poring over the records, the researchers found that a Mogul balloon had been launched on 4 June 1947. Critically, this balloon had been lost by the tracking radar and it had never been found – at least not officially. According to the new USAF theory, the wreckage found by Brazel was of this new and top secret Mogul balloon launch. It was for this reason that those who handled it at Roswell thought that it was new and unusual and most definitely not a weather balloon. They were correct.

MOGUL BALLOON

The Mogul balloon would have consisted of two parts. First there was the gas-filled balloon which provided the lift. Second there was the payload which contained the equipment. Unfortunately the detailed records of precisely what this particular launch contained have not survived so nobody can be certain of what it was composed.

If it were a typical Mogul launch, however,

▶ A rare photograph of a Mogul balloon. In 1947 the existence of these balloons was top secret.

the balloon would have been a polyethylene giant. Trailing from the bottom of it would have been a cable some 200 ft (60 m) long. Attached to this at intervals would be the individual components of the payload. In addition to the secret equipment, it would have included three or more folded parachutes designed to float the equipment to earth if the cable snapped, two or more aluminium radar reflectors and other bits and pieces.

The polyethylene fabric was new in 1947, unlike the rubber used to manufacture the much smaller balloons that carried aloft weather recording equipment. It would have been unfamiliar to all those at Roswell who handled it. Also relatively new was the material used to make the radar reflectors. This was a thick paper coated with aluminium that was considerably stronger and easier to handle than aluminium foil. Again this would probably have been new to those who encountered it. It is argued by the USAF report that these factors taken together would have been enough to convince Brazel, Marcel and Blanchard that they had on their hands something very unusual indeed.

However, when the wreckage reached Ramey, he did recognize it for what it really was. Realizing that the media attention being given to the story threatened to reveal the existence of Project Mogul, Ramey then concocted the story about a weather balloon. The photos taken of the debris in Ramey's office certainly do show bits and pieces that could have come from a balloon, but do not include any of the top secret Mogul gear. It looked as if Major Marcel had been correct, or at least partially so. Ramey must have removed some of the debris before he allowed the press to see it. Whether or not he substituted other material the USAF researchers had no way of knowing. But quite clearly the wreckage shown to reporters was not the same as that transported to Fort Worth from Roswell by Marcel. Important parts of it – the parts that Marcel, Blanchard and Brazel

had considered to be the most odd – were almost certainly missing.

However, the men at Roswell did not just fail to recognize the crashed Mogul balloon; they went so far as to suggest that it was a flying saucer.

The report suggested that the confusion came about because the men concerned were unfamiliar with flying saucer sightings. It must be remembered that the Roswell Incident took place when 'flying saucers' were only just beginning to be reported and discussed. Today

> ## The polyethylene fabric was new in 1947, unlike the rubber used to manufacture the much smaller balloons that carried aloft weather recording equipment.

most people have an image in their minds of what a UFO looks like and how it behaves. Back in early July 1947 that was very far from being the case. These mysterious objects were only just beginning to be reported. Such sightings as had surfaced in the press described flying saucers as being metallic, fast-moving and utterly mysterious. So when Brazel found some strange metallic debris on his ranch, claiming it to be a flying saucer was not as unlikely then as it would be today.

Having thus explained the events surrounding the Debris Field as reported in contemporary newspapers, the report turned to the accounts linked to the Roswell Incident by later witness statements.

One of these was the description of the metallic debris found by Brazel as having remarkable properties. The most frequently reported property was that the metal foil could be scrunched up into a ball, whereupon it would spring back out to its original shape.

The aluminium paper used as the radar reflectors on Mogul balloons would not have acted like this. However, other secret launches sent up by the USAAF did include a material that behaved in a similar way. These were balloons that were used as targets for guided missiles using radar to home in on enemy aircraft.

These balloons were made of polyethylene coated with a thin covering of aluminium. The aluminium would give a radar response similar to that of an aircraft, while the balloon was both big enough for it to be seen from the ground if the missile hit home and cheap enough to be expendable in tests. A successful strike by a missile would blast the balloon to

pieces, scattering shreds of the material over a wide area. The material did, indeed, look metallic and, if rolled into a ball, would spring back to a flat shape again.

The problem was that this material did not enter service until 1948 and was not used extensively over New Mexico until 1955. However, in line with its views on the frailties of human memory, the report considered it likely that witnesses had remembered handling such odd material in the mid-1950s, but had mistakenly ascribed the incidents to the 1947 event.

The researchers then turned to reports of alien bodies. Assuming that the eyewitnesses

who reported seeing dead aliens had not been talking about July 1947, but had only placed their memory at that time in response to the excitement generated by the Roswell Incident, the researchers looked for events at around that time that might explain the reports.

They noted that most of the reports had certain features in common. The events generally featured a craft that had apparently crashed and which contained aliens. The aliens were usually reported to be lifeless. They were said to be humanoid in shape but not entirely human in appearance. Several accounts said the humanoids had only three fingers, or lacked a thumb. The aliens were

◀ A sheet of crumpled metal. Witnesses to the debris found at Roswell insist that it was a thin, metallic substance that would spring back flat when crumpled up.

also said to be bald or hairless and to be dressed in tight-fitting, one-piece outfits. Quite often the bodies were said to be found and hurriedly retrieved by military personnel arriving in jeeps or small trucks. The witnesses seemed to place the wrecks at two sites; one on the Plains of San Agustin (near Socorro) and a second to the north of Roswell.

EXPERIMENTS AT WHITE SANDS

It did not take the researchers long to realize that the reported crashed craft and alien bodies were said to have come down within 100 miles (160 km) of the White Sands Proving Ground. In the 1940s and 1950s White Sands was the site used by the USAF for test launches of experimental rockets, aircraft and other flying objects of many different types. Some of these were of very unconventional design and certainly did not resemble a standard aircraft of the time. Several of them could, especially if mangled by a crash, fit the description given of the supposed crashed alien spacecraft.

The presence of alien corpses at first seemed more of a challenge to explain. However, it soon emerged that among the top secret experiments carried out at White Sands

"Any object being used to test an ejection seat needs to be of the same size and weight distribution as the human pilot who would be using it.

were some that would today be viewed as distasteful and probably immoral. These involved strapping chimpanzees and monkeys into small compartments inside rockets or aboard experimental aircraft, then firing them off into the air. The unfortunate animals were attached to monitors that

recorded the physical effects on them of being sent aloft in such extreme circumstances. Inevitably many of the animals perished, often in conditions of great pain and distress. It was all in the name of scientific advance and at the time was considered perfectly acceptable by the scientists doing the work.

The report, however, concluded that none of these White Sands launches could have explained the reports of a crashed alien spacecraft. The reason for this was that, according to the official records of White Sands, none of their launches had come down either at San Agustin or near Roswell. The records showed that every single launch had either come down within the vast area covered by White Sands itself, or had been successfully destroyed in the air by the on-board self-destruct devices. These were always fitted so that if a device did go off course it could be destroyed before it came down to cause damage to civilian property or expose the secrets on board to the prying eyes of Communist agents thought to be in the area.

Not every experiment was suitable for the use of chimps or monkeys in place of humans. The first such experiments to be carried out at White Sands were for the development of ejection seats for the fast jet fighters then entering service in large numbers. Any object being used to test an ejection seat needs to be of the same size and weight distribution as the human pilot who would be using it. Animals did not fit these criteria, so what is now known as the crash test dummy was developed.

Known at the time as anthropomorphic dummies, these devices were articulated as if they were human bodies and were packed with sensors. They were, back then, typically made with a steel and aluminium skeleton overlaid with foam padding and covered with a skin of latex or plastic. These dummies remained a classified secret for some years and did not become familiar to the public

▶ Anthropomorphic dummies as used by the USAF during tests in the 1950s. It is alleged that civilians finding these in the desert may have subsequently mistaken them for dead aliens.

until the 1970s. It was considered likely that an average civilian coming across such an anthropomorphic dummy in the late 1940s or early 1950s would have been deeply puzzled and mystified by it. They might even have mistaken the dummy for a dead alien.

The problem for the USAF research was that, as with the launches involving animals, all of the tests of missiles or aircraft that had carried dummies were officially accounted for. None had fallen outside of White Sands.

There were, however, a series of tests that did see anthropomorphic dummies involved that ended with them scattered all over New Mexico. These were the tests designed to find a method of safely returning an astronaut to Earth from an orbiting spacecraft if that craft were to suffer a serious malfunction. The tests took many forms, but those of most relevance to Roswell were the 'high altitude balloon drops'. This involved taking dummies up to heights of around 100,000 ft (30,000 m) by balloon, and then dropping them. The drops were preformed to test two pieces of equipment.

The first was an automatically released parachute that was designed to open at a safe altitude whether or not the person wearing it was conscious. The second was the padded, cooled and ventilated outfit that would (after a few modifications) become the familiar spacesuit.

In the course of these tests the dummies frequently suffered minor damage. The researchers thought that this might account for the reports of hands with only four digits, oddly-shaped heads and the like.

The first of these tests was carried out in June 1954 and they continued through to February 1959. In all about 250 drops were carried out over New Mexico. The researchers concluded that these tests were the most likely source of the reports of dead aliens. Not all the parachutes opened properly, so some dummies plummeted straight to Earth. A few

others were not found immediately by the tracking team, giving the parachute time to become detached and blow away. One dummy was not found for three years after it was dropped and at least four have never been recovered.

As with the reported sightings of dead aliens, the dummies used in these tests would have been picked up by military teams under the command of junior officers who travelled in jeeps or small trucks. Any civilians who got in the way would have been firmly, though hopefully politely, steered away from the area and asked not to talk about anything that they had seen. It was also usual to take down names and addresses in case the military wanted to check out the civilians and eliminate them as potential spies.

> As with the reported sightings of dead aliens, the dummies used in these tests would have been picked up by military teams commanded by junior officers who travelled in jeeps or small trucks.

Although this was the USAF researchers' favoured explanation for the reports of dead aliens, it does not quite fit the facts. All the eyewitness reports say the bodies were lying close to or in a crashed flying craft. The eye-witnesses seem to be describing dummies used in missile or aircraft tests, yet the official records of White Sands insisted that this was not possible. The researchers believed these reports and so preferred the high altitude balloon drop explanation.

The report then moved on to look at some of the other reported events in some detail. One of the witnesses whose statements were dealt with in depth was Glenn Dennis. Dennis was the young man working at the Roswell

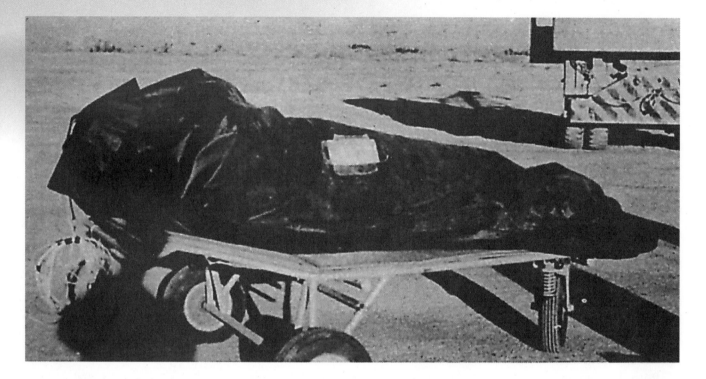

▲ The same body bags used for the retrieval of battlefield casualties were used to transport anthropomorphic dummies, which may have led witnesses to conclude that the dummies were bodies.

funeral parlour who recalled two sets of events, placing them in early July 1947.

Mysterious Nurse

The first of Dennis' recollections was of receiving a series of odd phone calls from Roswell air base asking his advice about acquiring caskets for child-sized bodies, followed by questions about preserving corpses that had been exposed to the desert air for some days. Dennis also recalled an incident at the base itself. He met a nurse whom he knew who told him about grotesque bodies recovered from the desert that were subjected to an autopsy despite the hideous smell that they emitted. Dennis reported that the nurse left Roswell abruptly soon afterwards and was later reported to have been killed in an accident in Britain. On the same visit to the air base, Dennis recalled being stopped by an aggressive red-headed officer who questioned his right to be on the air base, and then had him escorted off the base by military police.

The researchers knew that they would have

access to the personnel records of all those who had served in the USAAF at Roswell in 1947, so they set about tracking down the missing nurse and the red-headed officer. Dennis had at first said that the nurse's name had been Naomi Selff, but had later admitted that this was a fictitious name he had invented as he had promised the woman he would never reveal her name after she told him about the bodies. The researchers soon found that no nurse called Selff or anything similar had served at Roswell.

However, Dennis had given other information about the missing nurse. He said that she had been 'short with short black hair, dark eyes and olive skin', and that she was a Catholic from Kentucky. There had been such a nurse at Roswell in 1947. Nurse Lieutenant Eileen Fanton matched the physical description given by Dennis and was a Catholic from Kentucky. She left Roswell without notice in September 1947. There was, however, nothing suspicious about her departure. She was diagnosed as suffering from a medical condition that required hospital treatment. When she was again passed fit for duty she was reassigned, not back to Roswell but to Britain, as Dennis had claimed.

The only discrepancy between the missing nurse and Eileen Fanton was that Fanton did not die in an accident in Britain. However, Dennis' only evidence for this fatal accident befalling his missing nurse was that he had had a letter he wrote to her in Britain returned to him marked 'deceased' and that he later heard a rumour. There may be an explanation. In 1947, Fanton was an attractive, young, single woman who, by Dennis' own account, had grown close to the handsome young mortician. It is not beyond the bounds of possibility that, having moved to a new base, and no doubt having struck up new friendships and relationships, Fanton no longer wanted to be bothered by a young man from her past. Perhaps she had the letter returned herself. She died before she could be interviewed.

The tall red-headed captain could not be identified as readily as the missing nurse. There had been a tall red-headed colonel based at Roswell. This was Colonel Lee Ferrell who commanded the hospital and medical services on the base from 1954 to 1960. His dates of service at Roswell would seem to rule him out as the man mentioned by Dennis as being present in 1947. However, in his various accounts, Dennis also mentioned other USAF personnel by name who played no real role in the Roswell Incident, but whom Dennis placed on the base at the time. Of these, neither Captain Lucille Slattery nor Captain Frank Nordstrom were at Roswell in July 1947. Slattery arrived in August 1947 and Nordstrom in June 1951.

These dates raise the possibility that the incident of the red-headed officer aggressively questioning Dennis when he found him in the hospital took place not in 1947, but at some time during Ferrell's time there. The USAF researchers looked at the various versions of the story told by Dennis and concluded that the incident had involved three or more black, grotesque bodies that emitted an unpleasant smell being brought into the air base hospital for a post-mortem. Dennis also claimed that one or more officers from off the base had arrived to perform the autopsy and that the procedure had been carried out under conditions of greater security than was usual. One of the bodies had a head larger than was normal for a human, and it had been taken to Wright Field. Dennis said that he had seen a truck containing purplish or bluish wreckage marked by hieroglyphs or foreign writing. Finally,

> **USAF researchers concluded that the incident had involved three or more black, grotesque bodies that emitted an unpleasant smell being brought into the air base hospital for a post-mortem.**

Dennis said that he was ejected from the base on the orders of a tall red-headed officer.

Astonishingly, the researchers found an incident that more or less matched these facts, but it had taken place in 1956, not 1947. On 26 June a four-engined KC-97 air refuelling transport plane took off from Roswell with a fully loaded fuel storage tank in its fuselage. Eight miles (13 km) south of Roswell a propeller sheared off an engine on the KC-97. The propeller blade flew through the fuselage side, pierced the huge fuel tank and ignited the aviation fuel. The aircraft exploded in a massive fireball and wreckage was scattered over a large area. All 11 crew members were killed instantly by the blast.

The bodies were recovered over the following 24 hours and taken to the Roswell air base hospital. They were badly burned and blackened, grotesquely deformed and smelled

appalling. Red-headed Colonel Ferrell imposed tight security, ordering that 'no information will be divulged concerning identification or shipment [of the bodies] until a final determination of identity has been resolved for all remains'. He took personal control of security at the hospital. Because the remains were so badly burned and mangled by the crash, Ferrell sent for a specialist in the identification of human remains. When the identification was over, the bodies were flown off base.

> **Because the remains were so badly burned and mangled by the crash, Ferrell sent for a specialist in the identification of human remains.**

The match to the incident described by Dennis is close, but not exact. It was good enough for the USAF researchers to conclude that Dennis had remembered the disturbing incident fairly accurately, but had mistakenly placed it in 1947.

The accounts given by other witnesses were subjected to similarly detailed analysis and attempts were made to explain what was seen in terms of routine or secret military activity in the area. With varying degrees of confidence, the USAF report explained away the statements made by most of the witnesses who had come forward to speak in public, and whose accounts are given in this book.

The reaction given to the USAF report was mixed. Sceptics seized on it as a comprehensive explanation of what had happened and used it to discredit not only the Roswell Incident but UFOs in general. Some UFO researchers were also convinced. They tended to be those not directly involved in investigating the incident or those who had themselves noticed discrepancies in the various accounts of the alleged crashed saucer. William Moore, the co-author of the first book on the alleged Roswell UFO crash, was one of those who changed his mind.

Other researchers were not convinced, pointing out that the USAF report was itself flawed and incomplete. It made no attempt to explain the major efforts made by the USAAF at the time to hush things up. When other Mogul balloons came down, the civilian finders were paid their reward and then left alone. They were not subjected to threats either real or implied, as at Roswell. Nor was the report's explanation of anthropomorphic dummies dropped from balloons entirely convincing given that all the witnesses who reported the dead aliens said that they were in or close to a crashed flying craft of some kind.

Above all the USAF explanation rested almost totally on the assumptions that official documentation could be trusted absolutely but that the memories of civilians could not. One does not need to be an obsessive believer in conspiracy theories to suspect that while the latter proposition might well be true, the former is not always the case.

Meanwhile, the Roswell story continued to unfold despite the efforts of the USAF to explain it away.

9

Big Business
in Roswell

▶ The town of Roswell now has street lights shaped to resemble an alien's head, a sign of the importance of the Roswell Incident to the town's economy.

ON THE DAY THAT Mac Brazel set out to take his box of unusual debris into Roswell, it was a quite unremarkable small town, just like a hundred others spread across the arid south-western states. If it had not been for the 509th Bomber Group stationed nearby, it is unlikely that anyone outside of New Mexico would have heard of the place. But Brazel's actions were to change all that.

The name of Roswell was catapulted into the national and international headlines for a few hours, then just as suddenly forgotten – at least by most. But the story of a crashed flying saucer simply refused to die. Throughout the 1980s and early 1990s the speculation about what had happened in July 1947 continued to grow; books were published and television shows produced. In 1994, a film starring Martin Sheen and Kyle McLachlan was made for television. Even the publication of the USAF report with its detailed study of the reports and witness statements failed to quieten the fuss.

In some ways Roswell is today not very different from the small town of 1947. It is still a centre for dairy farming, sheep ranching, small scale manufacturing and irrigation farming. Its largest place of employment is a factory making mozzarella cheese – the largest such facility in the world. Its population of around 46,000 is considerably larger than in 1947, but it is still ranked among the many small towns of the USA. Several of the buildings in Main Street are those that stood there in 1947. Now, as then, it is the capital of Chavez County and houses the county fire service, sheriff and other local government offices.

AIR BASE CLOSURE

In other ways the place has changed considerably. It gained a spark of showbiz glamour when a girl born there went on to become the

▲ Hollywood actress Demi Moore came from Roswell.

Hollywood star Demi Moore, and a touch more when a local boy gained fame as country singer John Denver. In 1967 the economy of the town took a major hit when the nearby USAF base closed down. Known as Roswell Army Air Force Base in 1947, and later as Roswell Air Base, it was renamed Walker Air Base in 1948. At its height thousands of service personnel were stationed there. Their off-duty spending was a huge

> The name of Roswell was catapulted into the national and international headlines for a few hours, then just as suddenly forgotten – at least by most.

boost to the economy of the town and their departure has never really been replaced. The site of the base is now a civilian airport which goes by the name of Roswell International Air Center, but which has no scheduled international flights. Today the average income of the Roswell population is below the national average, and rather more of the households fall below the poverty line than is the case nationally. Despite this, Roswell is not a poor place and presents a well-kept and orderly face to the world.

No visitor to the town can hope to escape the UFO heritage of the place. Motels and shops have names featuring aliens and saucers, UFOs and other planets. The most famous of all the UFO-related sights is the Roswell International UFO Museum and Research Centre, which opens its doors to visitors all through the year apart from Thanksgiving, New Year and Christmas. The museum has a lively site on the internet at http://www.roswellufomuseum.com, through which it sells a wide array of gifts, souvenirs and clothing – all with a UFO or alien link.

Located at 114 Main Street, the museum was founded by Glenn Dennis and Walter Haut, both of whom have been key witnesses. Their accounts are featured elsewhere in this book. Since it opened in 1992, the museum has attracted an increasing number of visitors. It claims to have been the chief inspiration behind what has now become a big business in Roswell – the celebration of the alleged UFO crash in 1947. Many local businesses feature aliens or UFOs on their company logos, and even the city council has got in on the act with street lights designed to resemble alien eyes.

UFO FESTIVAL

In 1996 the museum joined forces with the Roswell Chamber of Commerce to stage a 'UFO Festival' on the anniversary of the alleged crash. The event was a great success and has been held every year since on the weekend closest to 4 July. Thousands of visitors and locals flock to the event, which includes a carnival parade and alien costume contest for the younger fans through to serious lectures on aliens and UFOs for the more

grown-up visitors. The weekend is now one of the premier tourist attractions in New Mexico.

There can be no doubt that the Roswell crash has become a major boost to the local economy.

It has also reached out to touch many areas of popular culture in the USA and abroad.

Writer Melinda Metz has produced a series of teenage novels based on the idea that four of the teenagers at the local Roswell High School are, in fact, alien-human hybrids sent to Earth as cloned replacements for the royalty of Antar, an alien planet. This 'Royal Four' will one day return to Antar to save their race.

▲ A scene inside the Roswell UFO Museum, which contains many artefacts relating to the alleged 1947 crash.

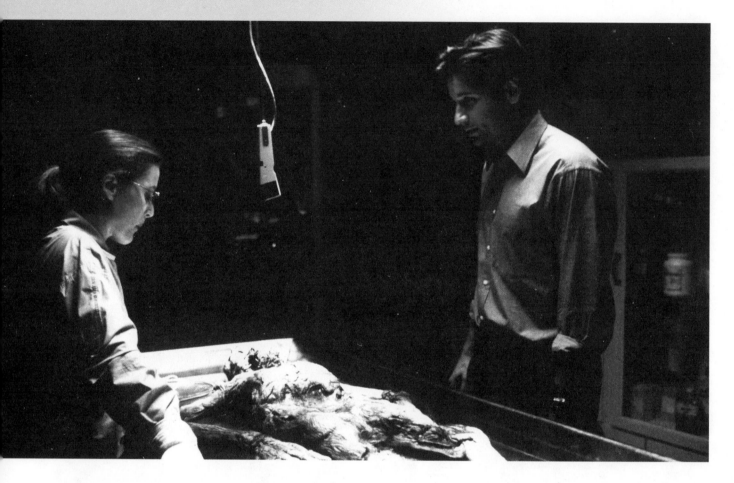

▲ Events at Roswell in 1947 – real, alleged and imagined – have featured in numerous movies and TV shows. This scene is from the television series, *The X-Files*.

Central to the ongoing plot of the novel series are the relationships between the hybrids and their human companions. In 1999 the books were launched as a TV series that aired for three seasons.

The incident has been used in numerous other books and shows, testifying to the fact that the producers expect the audience to understand the references made. An episode of *Star Trek: Deep Space 9* has a group of Ferenghi aliens catapulted backwards in time to 1947 and crash-landing their spacecraft near Roswell. An episode of the comedy cartoon *Futurama* likewise had an episode in which its characters crashed at Roswell in 1947. Roswell has also been mentioned in television shows such as *The X-Files*, *Stargate SG1*, *Taken*, *Dr Who* and even the children's Disney show *Buzz Lightyear of Star Command*.

Some scientists who deal with folklore and anthropology have produced papers that proclaim the Roswell Incident to be a modern folk tale or folk myth in the making. The way in which the story has been taken up in fictional television shows or books is clear evidence of how the underlying claims are being manipulated and changed for entertainment. Rather more controversial are the suggestions that the ongoing investigations by serious researchers into the events are subjected to the same myth-making process.

CHANGING VIEWS

It is certainly true that the reconstruction of events postulated by researchers has changed over the years. According to the researchers this has happened as new witnesses have been found or old ones have been shown to have questions around their accounts. A typical

example might be the stories told by Barney Barnett. When the investigations into the Roswell Incident began in the later 1970s, Barnett's evidence was treated seriously and featured prominently in all accounts. By the later 1980s, Barnett's evidence was being relegated to secondary importance and by the late 1990s was mostly ignored.

Researchers point out that Barnett had died some years earlier, meaning that his testimony was second-hand and could not be subjected to cross-examination. His evidence had been useful in putting together the outline of the event and in drawing out new witnesses, but was of only secondary credibility and so had been dropped when new evidence by witnesses still living had come forward.

Sceptics would have responded that the reason Barnett's testimony was ignored in later studies was that it no longer fitted with the emerging 'truth' as stated by those who believed that an alien spacecraft had crashed at Roswell. Barnett had put the crash he witnessed on 'The Flats', a phrase usually taken to mean the Plains of San Agustin though it could be argued that he had meant any large area of flat ground. By the late 1980s, however, the alien spacecraft was believed to have crashed in broken country just north of Roswell. Barnett's testimony did not fit, so it was ignored.

The supermarket in Roswell has a painting of a saucer flying through the outer solar system on its exterior wall.

The way in which the story has been taken up in fictional television shows or books is clear evidence of how the underlying claims are being manipulated for entertainment.

Similarly, the evidence given by Bessie Brazel, Mac Brazel's daughter, was on the face of it just as credible as that given by her brother Bill. Both were alive to be interviewed and cross-examined when the investigation began in the late 1970s, and both were in fact interviewed several times during the 1980s. However, most books feature Bill's testimony prominently but ignore Bessie's. One reason given for this is that in 1947 Bill was an adult, while Bessie was only 14 years of age. True enough, but it is also the case that Bill spoke at length about finding some very odd wreckage, while Bessie thought it was just a heap of old rubber, paper and other rubbish.

Those wanting to get some recognition

> **Those wanting to get some recognition have spilled much ink declaring the Roswell Incident to be a developing folk myth, while researchers have hit back at them with gusto.**

have spilled much ink declaring the Roswell Incident to be a developing folk myth, while researchers have hit back at them with gusto. All of this helps to keep Roswell and the events alleged to have happened there in the public eye. They contribute nothing, however, to understanding of the events.

Others have entered the field with their own ideas. In 1997 the Austrian Rene Coudris published a book putting forward his own ideas. Coudris is the Director of the Institute for Transcommunication and Metapsychology in Salzburg. Prior to his writing *The Roswell Message*, his best-known work had been a book recording his telepathic communications with his unborn child while it was still in its mother's womb.

In his work, Coudris set out in great detail his telepathic communications with beings that claimed to be aliens, and who claimed to come from the race which had sent the spacecraft that crashed at Roswell. The aliens told Coudris that they had come from a planet named Asastan that lay some 750 million light years away, and that they were about 3 million years more advanced in evolutionary terms than humans. After giving some details about the crash – that the spacecraft had had a crew of three, two of whom were named Bax and Alira – the aliens went on to claim that they were well disposed towards humans. However, humanity was headed for disaster and it was the mission of the aliens to warn humans of this. Unfortunately the warnings were too vague to be of much use in averting the catastrophe.

REDFERN'S THEORY

In 2005 a rather less bizarre theory emerged in the work of Nick Redfern. Redfern highlighted a fact overlooked by other researchers – that a large prisoner of war camp had been located at Roswell during the Second World War. Some of the German prisoners there built a large stone 'Iron Cross' which is now something of a tourist attraction in its own right. There were also large numbers of Japanese internees and prisoners held at Roswell, and it was on these that Redfern focused.

According to Redfern, the US military used some of the Japanese prisoners for experi-

▲ The stone cross erected at Roswell by prisoners of war kept there during World War II.

ments at White Sands involving the testing of revolutionary new aircraft designs. Among these were the flying wing and flying disk designs of the German Horten brothers, plans of which had been taken from Germany's Luftwaffe research facilities when the Third Reich was defeated in 1945. Another experimental craft was an advanced balloon based on the Japanese Fugo designs. According to Redfern two of these test flights ended in catastrophic crashes in which the crews were killed. A Fugo had crashed at the Foster Ranch, while a Horten wing had come down near Socorro. These two crashes, Redfern argued, were the basis for the eyewitness accounts of aliens and crashed spacecraft.

It was unfortunate for Redfern's ingenious theories that much of his best evidence came in the form of testimony from people claiming to have been involved in the experiments, but who wanted to remain anonymous. This has made it impossible for other researchers to check out their stories; nobody has been able to find out if they really did hold the posts that they claim to have held and whether or not they were at White Sands in 1947. Redfern's theories remain unproven and, it must be said, not widely accepted.

There can be no doubt that Roswell will continue to benefit economically from its links to the alleged UFO crash. And people other than Coudris and Redfern will come forward with new theories and ideas, and with books to sell.

Whatever it was that crashed at Roswell in 1947 has become big business.

Conclusion

MY AIM AT THE START of this book was to unearth the truth behind the Roswell Incident, and to this end I have done my best to lay out the known truth in a clear, balanced way. I have sought to explain why some pieces of evidence have been treated seriously while others have not. In an effort to give you all the facts so that you, the reader, can reach your own conclusions, I have even included witness testimonies that most researchers have dismissed as discredited.

I have written numerous books about what might be loosely termed 'unexplained phenomena', ranging from UFOs to ghosts and poltergeists. But the events of that July evening are unlike any I have investigated previously.

Of the many hundreds of UFO reports that I have investigated, none come close to Roswell. It simply does not fit the pattern.

While many people might be sceptical about the existence of UFOs, from my research it is clear that witnesses who report sightings of them generally describe objects that are consistent with other such reports. Some think UFOs are natural phenomena perhaps linked to atmospheric plasmas, others consider them to be alien spacecraft; a few link them to traditional tales about fairies and gods, while others dismiss the entire subject as nonsense.

But Roswell was and is totally different. The flying craft involved crashed, which UFOs do not generally do, and it left behind very solid pieces of wreckage. Of the many hundreds of UFO reports that I have investigated, none come close to Roswell. It simply does not fit the pattern.

But just because Roswell was atypical, that does not mean that it could not have been a UFO as we now think of them. Many UFO sightings are odd to the point of being unbelievable, and yet they happened. It is important to bear in mind what was known to the people involved in the Roswell Incident.

When the object crashed at Roswell in July 1947, the whole subject of flying saucers or UFOs was very new. At that date most people did not have a clear image in their minds of how a UFO should appear, still less of what the aliens who piloted them should look like. Sceptics argue that in the summer of 1947 a rancher finding something very odd that had fallen from the sky on to his land might declare it to be a 'flying saucer' when all he really meant was that the object was very peculiar and futuristic.

Under this scenario, the explanation for the Roswell Incident would go something like this:

At the time everyone agreed that there was something odd about the wreckage found by Mac Brazel. However, if it had been as bizarre and peculiar as pieces of an alien spacecraft might be expected to be, then the journalists who spoke to Brazel would undoubtedly have said so. They did not. What Brazel found was, as he said, unlike anything he had ever seen before but it was within the bounds of possibility given the technology of the time. It was odd, but not obviously alien.

All the descriptions that we have of truly bizarre material – super-strong metal foil that can be crushed but not cut, bent but not folded and which always sprang back to its original shape – come from witness statements made decades after the event. It is possible that memories have become confused, exaggerating the properties of the material or confusing it with metal-coated plastic used by the USAF in the 1950s – and fragments of which are known to have fallen on New Mexico during tests. Even if the reports are taken at face value, they are describing something very odd but which still falls short of the level of strangeness that could fairly be expected of wreckage from an interplanetary craft.

Sceptics would argue that, all things considered, it is most likely that what Mac Brazel found was the wreck of a Mogul balloon. The descriptions given at the time are in line with this, and the witness statements recorded later are not entirely inconsistent. It would certainly explain all the contemporary accounts, and why General Ramey moved so quickly to hush things up.

But this would ignore the fact that several experienced and senior USAF officers were convinced, as was Brazel, that they had something very peculiar on their hands. The electronics dangling from a Mogul balloon might have been top secret and highly advanced, but the balloon itself was fairly conventional in construction. Yet Marcel, Blanchard and others recognized it as being something new and different. The fact that all descriptions of this futuristic material were written down years after the event does not necessarily invalidate them. Details might become confused, but the overwhelming impression gained is that everyone who handled the material was so struck by how odd it was that they remembered this fact clearly thirty or forty years later.

Then there are the stories about a crashed craft and alien bodies. The witnesses are consistent in describing finding humanoid bodies in or alongside a crashed craft of odd and unusual design. The USAF report suggested that anthropomorphic dummies used in various tests were responsible for the reports – yet the dummies were never used in flight tests of craft so different from a conventional aircraft that witnesses could mistake it for a flying saucer.

Furthermore, we know that several of the witnesses who claim to have seen crashed craft and bodies together were treated in a much harsher way than was normal. Witnesses who found dummies or crashed balloons were routinely rewarded with cash, but asked to keep quiet on grounds of national security. They were not threatened, cajoled or locked up.

There can be little doubt that the witnesses were substantially telling the truth about what they saw. They did see crashed craft with dead bodies. They did see US military personnel turn up to take control of the situation. They were threatened and intimidated into silence.

Where these witness statements do fall down is that none of those treated by all researchers as being credible and unbiased firmly link the crashed craft with bodies to the same date in July 1947 that Brazel found the strange debris on his land. The best that can be said is that the crash was seen in the summer of 1947, and not everybody is sure about that.

The witnesses are consistent in describing finding humanoid bodies in or alongside a crashed craft of odd and unusual design.

This point is crucial. If the strange debris, the crashed craft and the dead bodies all belong to the same incident then it is strange beyond belief. So strange, in fact, that the idea that this was a crashed alien spacecraft becomes as reasonable an explanation as any of the tortuous scenarios put forward by sceptics. But if the events are separate, then the individual elements become rather easier to explain away by conventional means.

Another point about the date is that if UFOs are alien spacecraft, then the Roswell Incident occurred within a few weeks of the aliens beginning large-scale visits to Earth. At the time it was speculated that the reason why an alien spacecraft might have crashed at Roswell was because of the powerful and, for the time, highly sophisticated radar and electronic equipment being used by the USAAF in the area. Most modern researchers have dismissed this idea on the grounds that an alien spacecraft would be of such advanced design that it would not be affected by mundane, 20th-century Earth technology.

But that misses the point. Alien technology would by definition be very strange and odd to us. Perhaps the motive power of their spacecraft – whatever that is – would be affected by a powerful radar beacon. We just don't know.

For what it is worth, I think that the USAF did cover up something that happened in New Mexico in the late 1940s or early 1950s. I don't believe it was a mere Mogul balloon. I think it was something much more important and much more serious. Everything points that way. But I don't know what it was. Perhaps it was a crashed alien spaceship. Perhaps it was a USAAF experiment that had gone horribly wrong.

Maybe one day the still-secret files will be opened up and we shall know the truth. Or maybe the facts have been expunged from the written records so effectively that the truth is lost forever.

It would not be the first time.

Appendix A
List of Characters

Studying the mosaic of information given by the various sources of information and using it to attempt to produce a coherent account of what is claimed to have happened in and around Roswell in July 1947 can be a complex business. In particular, remembering all the different people involved can be difficult. I therefore provide this list of those mentioned in this book.

Gerald 'Gerry' Anderson came forward in the 1990s giving a detailed and comprehensive account of events at Roswell that he claimed to have witnessed for himself. It later emerged that Anderson had been only 5 years old at the time and there was no evidence that he had, as he claimed, been with his uncle in Roswell in July 1947.

Pete Anaya and his brother Ruben were civilian workers at Roswell air base and had security passes to enter the outer compound of the base with its living areas, storerooms and hospitals. Pete claims to recall the events of July 1947 clearly and although he did not see much himself claims to be able to remember accurately what other people more closely involved told him at the time.

Grady 'Barney' Barnett was, in 1947, a civil engineer working on projects across New Mexico, but based in Socorro. He died before

UFO researchers became interested in the Roswell Incident, but had told of his experiences to friends several times. These accounts were consistent and clear, though in places rather vague.

Bessie (or Betty) Brazel is the daughter of Mac Brazel. Aged 14 in 1947, she claims to have seen and handled some of the wreckage.

William 'Mac' Brazel was the rancher on whose land the 'Debris Field' was found. He was quoted in the press at the time and spoke about the event to his friends and neighbours. Brazel died in 1963 so his testimony survives only as the second-hand accounts remembered by others and in documents written in 1947.

William 'Bill' Brazel Jr is the son of Mac Brazel. He was a young adult in 1947. He remembers some events that he experienced himself, and also recalls much of what his father told him about the Roswell Incident.

Glenn Dennis was, in 1947, an employee of the Roswell funeral parlour. His evidence is usually divided into two. The 'early version' was told by Dennis to many people over the years, while the 'late version' was told by Dennis only after the Roswell Incident became famous. By the 1990s, Dennis was running the profitable UFO Museum in Roswell.

Barbara Dugger is the granddaughter of Sheriff George Wilcox and his wife Inez. She did not witness anything herself, but claims that her grandparents told her much about what happened in July 1947 before they died.

Edwin Easley was the major in charge of military police at Roswell air base in July 1947. When first interviewed by researchers he denied that anything unusual had occurred in the summer of 1947. He later changed his story and claimed to remember an extensive military police operation.

Arthur Exon was stationed at Wright Field USAAF base in 1947. He saw very little himself, but claims to have spoken to many other servicemen who were involved with the Roswell event and says in his evidence that he clearly remembers what they told him. He came forward as a witness in the 1980s.

Walter Haut was the press officer at Roswell air base in 1947. It was Haut who issued the key press release announcing that a saucer had been captured. The evidence he gave early in the investigation was both consistent and impressive, though his role had been limited. Haut was later to become a more controversial witness as some researchers who interviewed him in his old age claimed that he had revealed new secrets, while others thought that by this time Haut was becoming frail and confused.

Curry Holden was a professor of history at the Texas Tech University. His presence at Roswell in July 1947 is disputed by some but accepted by others.

Frank Kaufmann served in the USAAF during the Second World War. He left in 1945, but claims that for some years afterwards he would work for the USAAF on and off on a temporary basis. He claims that in July 1947

he was working at Alamogordo air base and later at Roswell.

Major Jesse Marcel was the intelligence officer at Roswell air base in July 1947. It was his recollection of events that sparked the modern interest in the alleged saucer crash. Marcel has told his story many times to researchers and on television. Although there have been a few discrepancies in his evidence – and these have been seized on by sceptics – his main allegations and story have remained consistent.

Jesse Marcel Jr is the son of Major Marcel. He was aged 11 in 1947 and was involved only at the periphery. He claims to recall the events that he witnessed himself very clearly.

Floyd and Loretta Proctor were 'neighbours' of Mac Brazel, though their house was about 10 miles (16 km) away from his. They gave first-hand evidence about Brazel's actions and the debris that he found.

Robert Proctor is the brother of Floyd Proctor. He was serving as a flight engineer with the USAAF at Roswell in July 1947.

William Proctor is the son of Floyd and Loretta Proctor. He was aged 7 in July 1947.

Jim Ragsdale was a young man living near Roswell in 1947. He came forward with his story in the 1980s, but family members remembered him talking about it before then. In the 1990s, Ragsdale changed his story somewhat, adding more sensational details and claiming to have been present at events that he had earlier not mentioned.

Lewis Rickett was a sergeant in the Counter Intelligence Corps based at Roswell in July 1947. He came forward with his evidence in the 1980s.

List of Characters

Robert Shirkey was, in 1947, a lieutenant in the USAAF based at Roswell where he worked as an operations officer dealing with transporting supplies and other hardware.

Robert Slusher was a sergeant working alongside Robert Shirkey in 1947.

Robert Smith was a pilot flying C54 transport aircraft for the USAAF in July 1947.

Richard Tungate came forward in the 1990s. He joined the USAF in 1952 and claims that as a lieutenant he was assigned to Roswell on a temporary basis and then on a series of secret assignments. Some details of Tungate's story have been shown to be false, but researchers are divided as to whether or not this invalidates all of his claims.

Walter Whitmore Snr was the owner of KGFL, a radio station based in Roswell, in 1947. He died before the UFO researchers became interested in Roswell, but his evidence survives second-hand through his son, Walter Whitmore Jr.

Walter Whitmore Jr was one of the first witnesses contacted by researchers in the late 1970s. He gave an account of his father's involvement in the events of July 1947, and added some experiences of his own. He was in his early twenties in 1947.

George Wilcox was the sheriff in Roswell during 1947. Wilcox died before UFO researchers arrived in the 1980s. His evidence survives as contemporary documents and as remembered by his granddaughter Barbara Dugger.

Inez Wilcox was the wife of George Wilcox. Her version of events survives as remembered by her granddaughter Barbara Dugger.

There were numerous other witnesses involved in the Roswell Incident who have come forward, or been tracked down by researchers, over the years. Most of these have corroborating evidence to offer, rather than primary evidence. They are dealt with as they crop up.

Appendix B
Roswell Timeline

The timeline given here should be used with caution. It is an attempt to chart the various episodes alleged to have taken place in relation to the Roswell Incident in chronological order to aid the reader in understanding what happened when. However, it is by no means certain that all the events listed here actually happened in the way and at the time referred to – or that they ever took place at all. Some events rely only on the word of a single witness; others are said by different witnesses to have happened at different times. This is an attempt to bring some sort of order to the often confusing claims and counterclaims that have been made by the assorted witnesses and researchers.

1947

14 June

Possible date for crash of an alien spacecraft or a Mogul balloon near Roswell.

16 June

Possible date when Mac Brazel first sees debris on the Foster Ranch.

1 July

During the night: Radars at the USAAF bases at Roswell, White Sands and Alamogordo pick up unknown aircraft flying in the area.

2 July

Evening: A UFO is seen by some witnesses near Roswell. Possible date for crash of an alien spacecraft near Roswell.

3 July

Evening: A UFO is seen by some witnesses near White Sands. The launch of a V2 rocket is aborted at White Sands after a malfunction on the ground.

4 July

Evening: A UFO is seen by William Woody and his father near Roswell. Jim Ragsdale sees a UFO apparently diving towards the ground.

Evening: It is alleged by Frank Kaufmann that radar at Roswell picks up an unidentified aircraft flying erratically in the area. The object disappears suddenly from radar screens, indicating that it has landed or crashed.

Around midnight: A USAAF flight arrives at Roswell from Washington DC. The flight is allegedly unscheduled and arranged at short notice.

5 July

About 5 am: A team of scientists, apparently archaeologists, allegedly finds a crashed aircraft of unknown design on the ground north of Roswell. The archaeologists are allegedly joined by local man Barney

Barnett. Barnett later says that he saw small humanoid bodies at the Crash Site. Barnett later makes comments that indicate that the site may have been on the Plains of San Agustin, but might equally mean that it was on other plains elsewhere. One of the men heads for a phone to call the local sheriff's office. Sheriff George Wilcox takes the call and alerts the fire department, which sends a fire engine to attend the scene. Firefighter Dan Dwyer recalls travelling to a site about 35 miles (55 km) north of Roswell, not to the Plains of San Agustin. The crashed aircraft is not a design that he recognizes. USAAF officers then arrive and order the civilians to leave the Crash Site stating that it is a military matter that will be taken care of by the USAAF. This event may have happened on some other date.

About 7 am: Possible time when Mac Brazel first sees debris on the Foster Ranch. The extent and composition of the Debris Field is described differently in the various accounts. With Brazel, or called in by him soon after, is a second person, the identity of whom is disputed – possibly his neighbour William Proctor. Brazel collects some of the debris. Later that day he shows it to his neighbours Mr & Mrs Proctor (William's parents) and all agree that it is a strange material with properties unfamiliar to them. Mrs Proctor suggests that Brazel should take the debris to Sheriff Wilcox next time he is in town.

About 8 am: Radio reporter Johnny McBoyle tries to reach the site of a reported crashed aircraft. He is stopped by USAAF men and told the area is now off-limits to the public.

About 10 am: Glenn Dennis, working at a Roswell funeral parlour, receives the first of several phone calls from a contact at Roswell USAAF base making unusual inquiries. Dennis forms the impression that there has been a fatal accident at the air base, possibly involving an important person or secret piece of equipment.

Various times: A number of people from the Roswell area recall seeing armed guards sealing off an area of land north of Roswell. Details, times and other facts vary from witness to witness.

Afternoon: Glenn Dennis recalls arriving at Roswell USAAF base to be confronted by two officers he does not recognize and is ordered off the base.

Afternoon: It is alleged that alien bodies recovered from the crashed alien spaceship arrive at Roswell USAAF base. A preliminary medical examination, possibly by Dr Jesse Johnson, confirms that the bodies are non-human and are dead. The bodies are then placed in hermetically sealed containers.

Evening: It is alleged that the containers with the bodies are placed in a hangar, which is put under armed guard.

6 July

Morning: Mac Brazel arrives in Roswell to buy supplies and stops off at the sheriff's office. He shows the mysterious debris to Sheriff Wilcox. Presuming the debris may have come from an aircraft of some kind, Wilcox phones Roswell air base. The call is passed to intelligence officer, Major Jesse Marcel, who agrees to drive to town to talk to Brazel. Marcel is accompanied by another intelligence officer, Captain Sheridan Cavitt. What happens next is in dispute, but for some reason there is a prolonged delay before Brazel, Marcel and Cavitt set off for the Debris Field. They arrive in the late evening, so the military men are unable to observe much other than that there is a large amount of debris strewn over a pasture. According to some accounts, Brazel arrived in Roswell early on the morning of 7 July and Marcel raced to take him out to his ranch within minutes of being alerted to the fact he had found debris. Both accounts date the main search of the Debris Field by Marcel on the morning of 7 July.

7 July

Early morning: It is alleged that an unscheduled flight leaves Roswell air base for Andrews air base carrying samples of wreckage and at least one alien body.

About 5 am: Brazel, Marcel and Cavitt wake up at Foster Ranch and go out to inspect the Debris Field. What they find is disputed, but certainly enough debris to fill Marcel's jeep is collected. Marcel and Cavitt drive back to Roswell air base. It is probably at this point that Marcel stops at his home to show some of the debris to his wife and son.

Noon: Funeral parlour worker Glenn Dennis recalls meeting a friend who works as a nurse at Roswell air base for lunch. She seems upset and tells Dennis about a mysterious crashed aircraft and its unusual crew.

Afternoon: Lt General Nathan Twining, head of Air Materiel Command which includes Wright Field air base, lands at Alamogordo, allegedly after changing his plans at short notice.

8 July

Early morning: Marcel reports to Colonel William Blanchard, commander of Roswell air base, on his visit to the Foster Ranch. Blanchard alerts Major Edwin Easley and orders him to send a team of military police to collect all the debris from the Foster Ranch. It is disputed how much debris is collected, ranging in quantity from enough to fill a few boxes to several truck loads.

Morning: William Whitmore of local radio station KGFL records an interview with Brazel in Roswell about his finds. Whitmore recalls that he later received a phone call from a senior official in Washington DC advising him not to broadcast the interview, but cannot recall exactly when.

Morning: Brazel arrives at Roswell air base as requested by phone. He is taken to the guest house and left there under friendly guard.

11 am: Walter Haut, public relations officer at Roswell air base, is instructed by Blanchard to issue a press release announcing the capture of a 'flying disk'.

Noon: Haut arrives in Roswell to deliver copies of the press release by hand to the two newspapers and two radio stations in town.

Time uncertain: Sheriff Wilcox allegedly sends a deputy out to investigate further the aircraft crash reported a few days earlier. The deputy is turned back by military personnel before reaching the site.

2.26 pm: A message based closely on the press release issued by Haut is put out on the Associated Press (AP) wire service.

2.30 pm: Phone lines into Roswell air base are jammed by reporters trying to reach Haut. The avalanche of calls continues throughout the day.

About 2.30 pm: Blanchard announces that he is going on leave.

2.55 pm: The AP clears its international service to carry the report of 2.26 pm. Calls coming into Haut now include inquiries from foreign news media. Unable to get through to Haut, some reporters start calling the sheriff's office, the local newspapers and local radio stations. By about 4 pm all phone lines in and out of Roswell are jammed.

About 3 pm: Blanchard instructs Marcel to fly to Fort Worth, taking with him the debris collected from Brazel's ranch. He is to report to General Roger Ramey.

3.45 pm: Marcel arrives at Fort Worth and reports to Ramey with his boxes of debris. Ramey calls a press conference to take place at 6 pm. Exactly what happens next is disputed. Marcel says the debris is removed and replaced with pieces of a weather balloon; another officer present insists no such switch took place.

4.30 pm: It is announced that General Hoyt Vandenberg is taking control of the media operation regarding Roswell from the press room in the Pentagon, Washington DC.

5.30 pm: Reporters start arriving at Fort

Worth air base for Ramey's press conference. Major E. Kirton tells a reporter from the *Dallas Morning News* that the debris has been identified as coming from a weather balloon.

6 pm: Ramey's press conference begins. Warrant Officer Irving Newton (in charge of weather balloons at Fort Worth) is called in to identify the debris as being from a weather balloon. Ramey announces that the Roswell 'flying disk' is nothing but a weather balloon. Newton and Marcel are photographed with the debris.

6.17 pm: FBI agents send a teletype message to J. Edgar Hoover telling him that the USAAF is stating the Roswell flying disk to be a weather balloon.

7.30 pm: The AP wire service carries the announcement that the Roswell flying disk is a weather balloon. The number of calls coming in to Roswell from national and international media drops immediately.

10 pm: An unscheduled flight is alleged by Lewis Rickett to arrive in Roswell and is loaded with crates of pieces of the wreckage. It then departs for an unknown destination.

9 July

Morning: Local newspapers and radio stations carry the story that the 'flying disk' is only a weather balloon.

Morning: Sealed crates are seen being loaded on to a transport aircraft at Roswell air base. The aircraft leaves for Los Alamos.

Time uncertain: Bud Payne is chasing a stray cow on his ranch which is next to the Foster Ranch. He is suddenly stopped by military men in a jeep who turn him back saying that the area is temporarily off limits to civilians. The date of this event is not entirely certain.

Noon: One of the sealed crates in the hangar that allegedly stores pieces of the crashed flying saucer is moved to the highly secure and blast-proof bomb pit.

Around lunchtime: Brazel visits the local newspapers in Roswell to explain that what he found was a weather balloon. He is escorted by USAAF personnel. It is unclear if he is under arrest or not. Some accounts place this event on 10 July.

Afternoon: Two more transport aircraft leave Roswell allegedly carrying crates containing pieces of the flying saucer. One goes to Los Alamos, the other to Fort Worth. After the Fort Worth flight is unloaded it returns to Roswell air base with Marcel on board.

6 pm: Joseph Montoya, Lieutenant Governor of New Mexico, pays a visit to Roswell air base for unspecified reasons. When he returns he is clearly disturbed, refuses to discuss what he has seen and drinks heavily for the rest of the evening.

8 pm: Marcel arrives back at Roswell air base. He asks to see the intelligence reports and logbook completed during his absence – as is normal – but is told the documents have been removed on orders from Washington.

10 July

Morning: USAAF personnel call on Sheriff Wilcox and ask for the box of debris that Brazel had brought in on the morning of 6 July. Wilcox hands it over. Some time later, possibly a day or so afterwards, a USAAF sergeant calls and warns Wilcox that Glenn Dennis has seen things about which he should keep quiet and asks him to pass on the warning.

Daytime: Brazel is allegedly still held on Roswell air base.

11 July

Daytime: Glenn Dennis claims that he phoned Roswell air base to speak to his nurse friend, only to be told that she has been posted elsewhere at short notice.

Daytime and for several days: Several people say they recall receiving visits from military personnel asking them not to talk about recent events in and around Roswell.

12 July

About lunchtime: Brazel's son, Bill, claims that he travels to the Foster Ranch to fill in for his father while he is absent. There is no sign of any debris on the ground or military personnel when he arrives. He later finds a few pieces of debris in and around his father's house.

15 July

Mac Brazel returns to his ranch. He tells his son that he has taken an oath not to talk about the recent events. Brazel later repeats this to neighbours and friends.

Autumn 1947

Glenn Dennis claims to receive news that his nurse friend has been killed in an accident while stationed in or near London, England.

1949

Bill Brazel mentions in a bar that he still retains a few scraps of material recovered from the Debris Field. Next day, USAAF personnel arrive and confiscate the material.

1978

Jesse Marcel decides to speak out to tell UFO researchers of his experiences at Roswell in 1947. He is convinced that the weather balloon story was an orchestrated cover-up to conceal what really happened. Marcel tells UFO researcher Stanton Friedman that he believes that it was an alien spaceship that crashed at Roswell. Friedman begins investigations.

1980

The research produced by Friedman forms the core of the book *The Roswell Incident* written by Charles Berlitz and William Moore. This is the first comprehensive account to allege that an alien spaceship crashed at Roswell and that the US government covered up the fact.

1980s

Various witnesses come forward to give their version of events at Roswell in 1947 as they remember them.

1991

Publication of *UFO Crash at Roswell* by Kevin Randle and Donald Schmitt. This book pulls together the new evidence to give a more detailed account of the alleged crash, generally following the version in the 1980 book.

1992

Publication of *Crash at Corona* by Stanton Friedman. This book produces evidence that the Crash Site was as stated by Barnett, not Dwyer, and increases the body count to eight aliens. The controversial Majestic 12 documents are brought into the story for the first time.

1994

Randle and Schmitt respond with a revised version of their 1991 book, now entitled *The Truth about the UFO Crash at Roswell*. Differences of opinion over the date and location of the crash, together with how much credence could be given to different witnesses, come increasingly to the fore among researchers. The discrepancies have been much debated, but never properly resolved.

In July, a few weeks after Randle and Schmitt's revised book is published, the USAAF submit an internal investigation into the Roswell Incident to the Secretary of the Air Force. The report concentrates on documents (many of them still classified and unavailable to the public) that are held by the USAAF and other government bodies. The report announces that the official explanation used ever since 1947 – that the crash was that of a weather balloon – was an entirely false story concocted to cover up the truth. That truth, the report says, was that wreckage recovered had come from a secret USAAF project, code-named Mogul, that had used special balloons and equipment to spy on Russia. Response to the report is mixed, with sceptics hailing it as the final proof that no UFO had crashed, while UFO researchers points out discrepancies and ambiguities in the report.

1995

London-based science film agent Ray Santilli claims to have been offered a film of the autopsy carried out on one of the alien bodies recovered from the Roswell crash. He claims the film footage came from the USAAF cameraman who secretly kept a few minutes of film instead of handing it over to higher authorities. Some researchers accept the film as evidence that alien bodies were recovered from a UFO crash at Roswell, others denounce the film as a fraud; most reserve judgement until more evidence emerges.

2006

Controversy over the authenticity of the alien autopsy footage is revived when a comedy film, starring Anthony McPartlin and Declan Donnelly (Ant and Dec) is released purporting to show the way the footage was faked. Santilli subsequently admits the film was a hoax, but claims he had been hoodwinked by the true faker and is as much a victim of the fraud as everyone else.

Index

Index

Index